LIGHTS OF EAST ANGLIA

LIGHTS OF EAST ANGLIA

by

NEVILLE LONG

TERENCE DALTON LIMITED
LAVENHAM   .   SUFFOLK

1983

Published by
TERENCE DALTON LIMITED

ISBN 0 86138 028 2 hardback
0 86138 029 4 limp covers

Text photoset in 11/12pt. Baskerville

Printed in Great Britain at
The Lavenham Press Limited, Lavenham, Suffolk

Contents

TO KATHY

Foreword

THE material between these covers is the result of a fifteen-year labour of love by Neville Long. His work tells something of the story of The Trinity House, London, and the history and evolution of its lighthouses on the coasts of Norfolk, Suffolk and Essex.

In its history, The Trinity House has had its headquarters destroyed by fire in 1666, 1714 and 1940. As a result, many records and books have been lost and only by painstaking research (the reader will note the extensive appendix of sources and references) has the author been able to go a long way in completing the puzzle. I do not believe we will ever know why the Elder Brethren of the earlier centuries were slow to invoke the powers vested in them by their Monarch to establish seamarks. Mr Long has certainly done his homework and in many respects this volume is a tribute to the late Captain W. R. Chaplin, Elder Brother of Trinity House, London, from 1928 to 1974. Captain Chaplin, probably more than anybody, has put our records on a sound post-war footing and indeed the author has heeded his sound advice, "take your time and do the job thoroughly".

P. W. RIDGWAY
Public Relations Officer

Trinity House,
Tower Hill,
London EC3N 4DH.

Acknowledgements

IT might be imagined that all available information relating to an essentially maritime subject such as lighthouses would be found in the ports and seaside towns of our coastal counties. In fact, quite a lot of the evidence presented in these pages came to light in places far removed from the sea and scattered throughout the length, if not the breadth, of England. It is the result of a protracted and widespread search, in which the help and co-operation of a considerable number of public departments and individual persons had to be enlisted. It is pleasing to record that without exception this co-operation was freely and gladly given, and I welcome the opportunity to express my sincere thanks to all who were involved.

The foundations of this book were laid by the late Captain W. R. Chaplin, Elder Brother of Trinity House, London, and for many years its accredited lighthouse historian. It was Captain Chaplin who first arranged for me to have access to the surviving archives at Trinity House, and who not only spent many hours in helping me to sift through them, but kindly placed at my disposal the fruits of his own researches. The value of his contribution to the early stages of this project cannot be over-estimated. In the years since then I have continued to enjoy the utmost help and encouragement from Trinity House and I would like to tender my profound thanks to the Deputy Master and Elder Brethren, not least for allowing me to quote verbatim from their ancient books of Court Minutes. A special word of thanks is due to the Public Relations Officer, Mr Paul Ridgway, for reading and vetting the manuscript and for contributing the Foreword.

Out in the field, or perhaps I should say, out along the shore, my thanks are due to two successive Superintendents of the Trinity House Depot at Great Yarmouth, Captain S. A. Batte, T.H.S. (Retired), and the late Captain E. J. Lawrence. Both maintained a keen interest in this project and went to considerable trouble to ensure that I was kept informed of trends and changes taking place off the coast of East Anglia. My thanks are also extended to the full-time keepers and part-time attendants at the various east coast light stations, who suffered my frequent visits and answered my persistent questions. I am particularly indebted to Captain R. Dove, T.H.S., Chief Superintendent of the Trinity House Depot at Harwich, who provided much of the latter-day information contained in the final section.

I acknowledge with gratitude the practical assistance I received from the following official departments and organisations: The Department of the Environment; East Yorkshire Local History Society; King's Lynn Conservancy Board; King's Lynn Corporation; The National Maritime Museum; The

National Portrait Gallery; The Tate Gallery; The Public Record Office, London; the former East Yorkshire Record Office, Beverley; the Norfolk and Norwich Record Office; Suffolk Record Office, Ipswich; Essex Record Office, Chelmsford; the Berkshire Record Office, Reading; The British Library; the Guildhall Library and Fulham Central Library in London; and the provincial reference libraries of Bridlington, Hull, King's Lynn, Norwich, Ipswich and Saffron Walden.

I would also like to pay tribute to the photographic skills of Mr R. Jordan, of Gregory Studios, Norwich, Mr R. I. W. McRitchie, of West Norfolk Photographics, Hunstanton, and my former colleague, Mr D. J. Leech. Between them these three transformed an assortment of old prints, contemporary postcards and faded sketches into photographs suitable for reproduction.

Additionally, my warmest thanks are expressed to the following, all of whom have gone out of their way to be of assistance and whose order of mention below is purely alphabetical: Mr R. Emmerson, Arts Department, Norwich Castle Museum; Mr R. Gifford, Local Studies Section, Colchester Central Library; Mrs P. Gill, County Archivist, West Sussex Record Office; Mr V. Gray, County Archivist, Essex Record Office; Miss J. M. Kennedy, Archivist for the City of Norwich and County of Norfolk; Mr N. J. Marshall, Colman and Rye Local Studies Library, Norwich; Mr C. S. Minto, Central Public Library, Edinburgh; The Hon. R. H. C. Neville, of Audley End; Miss M. Ransome, Hon. Curator, Southwold Museum; Mr R. Trett, King's Lynn Museum; Mr A. Waters, Harwich Central Library; Mr Clive Wilkins-Jones, Colman and Rye Local Studies Library, Norwich; and Mr David Wright, Local Studies Section, Lowestoft Central Library.

It is quite possible, after such a prolonged period of preparation, that there is at least someone whose name I have omitted. If so, I crave their understanding, and their pardon.

NEVILLE LONG

Salhouse,
Norwich.
September, 1982.

Author's Note

This book concerns itself mainly with the past, so that details given here of lighthouses and other navigational aids may not hold true today. For this reason no information in these pages should be relied on for navigational purposes. Similarly the maps are intended as sketch-maps only and are not of navigational significance.

ix

Introduction

"No man will be a sailor who has contrivance
enough to get himself into a jail, for
being in a ship is like being in a jail
—with a chance of being drowned."
(Dr Samuel Johnson)

L ATTER-DAY generations have been raised in a society which devotes the utmost care and concern to the safety and preservation of life at sea. The slightest suggestion of trouble offshore, the fancied sighting of a flare or the most fleeting fragment of a radio call, is more than sufficient to spark off a full-scale search, with no expense spared and no risk untaken. Nowadays such behaviour is more than a mere code of ethics, it is an instinctive reaction.

So it is not easy to comprehend that there was a time when life at sea was regarded as cheap, expendable, and of very little consequence. Throughout the seventeenth century, and well into the eighteenth, safety standards were unknown, seaworthy ships something of a rarity and aids to navigation virtually non-existent. The outcome was an appalling loss of life at sea, which those with both feet safely on dry land accepted with almost total indifference.

These were the great years of expansion within the English coasting trade. This applied especially along the route between the Tyne and the Thames, where a fleet of countless sailing vessels kept up a shuttle service bringing coal to London and the East Coast ports.

Coal had now graduated from a new-fangled fuel to a vital necessity second only to the daily loaf. At the dawn of the seventeenth century a fleet of 200 colliers was needed to meet the demands of London alone.[1] By the end of that century a thousand sail of colliers and ten thousand seamen were employed in the seacoal trade.[2] It became the rule, rather than the exception, for fleets to leave the Tyne 300 or 400 strong. The casualty rate among them was enormous. In times of storm many were driven on shore or were cast away on the outlying sands. Not least among the dangers was that from the French and Spanish privateers who ranged far and wide over the North Sea. For this reason the coal ships hugged the coast, in the hope that pirate vessels would not venture close inshore. This did not always prove to be the case.

If the dangers were acute by day, they increased ten-fold with the coming of night. Coastwise navigation is utterly reliant on the recognition of conspicuous and familiar features on the land, and in the early days of sail it was just as important for the mariner to know the ups and downs of the coast as it was its ins and outs. The first primitive sea charts did not show the coastline from directly overhead, as is the case today. Instead they viewed it

Opposite: Lowestoft low light, built of iron
in 1866 and discontinued in 1923.

1

from an oblique angle, so that features such as cliff-faces, low-lying marshes, church spires and groups of trees were all identified. Nightfall rendered all these visual aids ineffective, and the colliers were left to grope their way uncertainly through inshore passages that were shallow, treacherous and, worse still, unlit. So there arose a vital and urgent demand for coast lights to indicate the danger spots and to enable the mariner to determine his position. Yet when the sixteenth century came to a close there was not a single lighthouse standing on the coasts of England.

There was nothing new in the concept of lighthouses. One of the seven wonders of the ancient world was a lighthouse, or pharos, which stood at the end of a causeway outside the harbour at Alexandria. The Romans made great use of lighthouses. Their route across the English Channel was marked by two beacons, one on the French coast near Boulogne and the other on the cliffs above Dover. The remains of this tower still stand in the grounds of Dover Castle. A good case can be argued in support of the belief that a Roman lighthouse stood on Flamborough Head, while in 1854 foundations of identical proportions to the tower at Dover were unearthed at Reedham in Norfolk.[3] It was at this point that the Yare once emptied itself into an extensive estuary.

At a later stage in history the display of coast lights became the self-appointed task of various monastic foundations. From the great abbeys and priories overlooking the sea coast, and from their smaller cells and outposts, down to the most lonely hermitage, candles shone out to light the way for passing ships. But with the dissolution of the monasteries by Henry VIII these early light-sources disappeared and the coasts were again in darkness.

The Elizabethan era was well into its stride before any further progress was made towards the safer navigation of our inshore waters. At last it came to be realised that seamarks were vital to the nation's trade and that if that trade was not to grind to an ultimate halt it was imperative that the coastline should be marked by day and lit by night. What the situation urgently demanded was that the responsibility for lights and seamarks should be vested in some specific administrating authority; a body well versed in the ways of the sea and uninfluenced by monetary considerations. Such a body already existed, in the form of an ancient guild of mariners with a history dating back to the reign of King John.

It would not be far from true to say that guilds were the mediaeval form of trade unions, although it required more than a mere subscription and a membership card for a man to become a member. He had to be master of his craft and possessed of a skill and knowledge born only of long years of experience. Guilds were powerful and exclusive, with strong religious ties. Most of them existed by right of a Royal Charter and they commanded a level of respect bordering on reverence. Some included in their official title the word "worshipful". It was a pretty fair description. Few professions today, except possibly Medicine and Law, are accorded quite such a degree of veneration as the craftsmen's guilds of the Middle Ages.

As might be expected in an island race, among the first of these foundations was a brotherhood of seafarers which, it was claimed, owed its origin to Stephen Langton, Archbishop of Canterbury during the reign of King John. Such fraternities seem to have come into being at four of the principal ports in the kingdom, Newcastle, Hull, Dover, and Deptford on the Thames. All had a common purpose and all appear to have been religious in concept. By the end of the fifteenth century these were well-established institutions. Three became corporate bodies bearing the name Trinity House under Charters granted to them by Henry VIII "out of the sincere love and likewise devotion which We have and bear towards the most Glorious and undividable Trinity."

It was the London branch of this foundation, the Trinity House of Deptford Strond, which was charged by Act of Parliament in 1566 with the responsibility for lights and seamarks. This Act related that, due to the destruction or removal of certain woods, steeples and other marks along the coasts, many ships had in recent years "miscarried, perished and been lost in the sea, to the great hurt of the Commonwealth and the perishing of no small number of People." By way of remedy the Act now gave sole power and authority to the Trinity House of Deptford Strond to erect and maintain "Beacons, Marks and Signs for the Sea" at such places along the coastline as they thought fit, "Whereby", the Act concluded, "the Dangers may be avoided and escaped and Ships the better come unto their Ports without peril."[4]

The immediate effect of this piece of legislation was precisely nil. It did not result, as might be expected, in an organised and efficient chain of lighthouses round our coasts, and the plight of those at sea did not improve to any extent. Trinity House existed at this time as a nautical, religious and charitable foundation with its headquarters in a large hall on Deptford Green. It was presided over by a Master, four Wardens and eight Assistants who were elected annually at a ceremonial gathering each Trinity Monday. All seafarers of English nationality were eligible to become Brethren, with the more senior among them enjoying the status of Elder Brethren. The many rights and privileges exercised by the fraternity included the licensing of Thames pilots and the sole right to sell shingle ballast dredged from the river bed. This lucrative source of income more than adequately financed the Corporation's other charitable activities, such as the care of aged and distressed mariners and the maintenance of its own almshouses.

So the years passed by until, by the beginning of the seventeenth century, private enterprise began to tire of the long delay in the provision of lights and seamarks. Men of wealth and influence were quick to appreciate the possibilities and exploit them to their own advantage. If the sailors valued their lives, the owners their ships and the merchants their cargoes, there should be no lack of support for anyone proposing to erect a lighthouse. And these same sailors, owners and merchants would not be averse to paying in return a prescribed rate of tolls, which would not only pay for the upkeep of the lighthouse but would yield a substantial dividend into the bargain.

For a private individual to establish a lighthouse it was first necessary to present to the sovereign a petition supported by the signatures of as many shipmasters, local dignitaries and merchants as possible, certifying that the light was needed and confirming their willingness to contribute tolls towards its upkeep. It became customary for the sovereign to forward these proposals

The arms of Trinity House.

to Trinity House for its recommendations. Invariably the Trinity Brethren opposed all these applications on the grounds that only they had the legal authority to erect seamarks. Their objections were overruled more often than they were sustained.

Throughout the seventeenth century successive monarchs, from James I to William III, persisted in favouring certain privileged persons with Letters Patent entitling them to erect lighthouses. For the Brethren of Trinity House it meant a hundred years spent in contesting numerous private projects, mostly for lighthouses along the east coast. It proved to be a century of mixed fortunes for the Brethren, who began by erecting their first lighthouse station at Caister near Yarmouth in 1600, and followed it nine years later with another at Lowestoft. They fought bitterly but unsuccessfully for Winterton, allowed Orford Ness to slip through their fingers and lost Hunstanton through under-estimating its importance. Worst of all, they were blatantly cheated out of Harwich by the double-dealings of no less a person than their own Master. On the credit side they were successful in thwarting a grandiose scheme to place lighthouses at a succession of points on the coast, from Corton in Suffolk northward to the Farne Islands. Finally, in 1680, they planted St Agnes lighthouse on the Scilly Isles before anybody realised exactly what was happening.

During the following century the drive to light the coasts gained in momentum, with Trinity House taking the initiative to a much greater degree. Few private petitions were submitted, fewer still met with any success. Instead of opposing new projects, Trinity House found itself concerned more with preventing existing leases from being renewed or extended. Very slowly the Brethren were gaining the upper hand, and their case was helped considerably by the growing public realisation that a handful of private persons were amassing substantial fortunes from lighthouses that were nowhere near as efficient, or reliable, as they should have been. Even so, it was many more years before positive steps were taken to eliminate the private ownership of lighthouses.

Throughout the era of private administration the individual patentees are fairly well documented and easily traced from one to another. Less so are the actual keepers, who seldom receive mention in anything more than mere name. Their duties were confined to stoking and watching the light, leaving matters of correspondence and accounting to the agent or overseer. The situation is made somewhat confusing by the fact that the agents themselves were often described as keepers. When we read, for instance, that in 1687 Thomas Wall and Thomas Willes kept the lights at Orford, we would be wrong to conclude that they were actively involved in tending the lights. They were, in fact, bailiffs of the town of Aldeburgh, to whom management and supervision of the station had been entrusted by the owner. Wall and Willes in turn employed two men to do the real work and these two were lightkeepers in the present-day understanding of the term. When, a few years later, John Hooke was appointed "keeper of the lights at Orford and at Winterton" his precise status becomes more obvious. Hooke may well have administered these places at one and the same time, but he would have been hard put to it to have tended both sets of lights simultaneously.

The lightkeeper's task was a servile and thankless one, often performed under conditions of great discomfort and difficulty. It entailed a good deal of heavy physical effort, both in manhandling coal up to the lantern platform and in trudging to and fro between the high light and the low. At the more lonely stations lightkeepers were continually at risk, and the prospect of sudden inundation by the sea was the least of their worries. Instances are recorded of lighthouses being attacked by foreign pirate vessels and of keepers being robbed of their possessions or carried off as prisoners. Some fared little better at the hands of their own countrymen, being snapped up by the press gang.

Lightkeepers worked interminable hours for minimal reward, which did nothing to foster any sense of loyalty to the owners who employed them or of moral responsibility to the sailors who relied on them. Cases of lightkeepers neglecting their duties or blatantly abusing their position are all too frequent. Some took advantage of a lack of supervision to supplement their income with other work during the day, arriving on duty in no condition to stay wakeful and vigilant throughout the night. Neglect of duty is one thing, but treachery is quite another, and the case which arose in June, 1691, must surely stand as the most deplorable, though fortunately isolated, incident of corruption in a lightkeeper. It was at the time of the war fought by England and Holland against the French, and the letter sent to the Secretary of State by the Commander-in-Chief of the Anglo-Dutch fleet is worth quoting in some detail:

"I am informed by several of the commanders of the cruising frigates that they have observed the officer of the lighthouse at Dungeness making

The Trinity House, seen in a Victorian print.

unusual fires at nights when any of our frigates are thereabouts, as a fire thrown to the eastward or westward of the lighthouse according as the frigates are from the lighthouse. Which they say upon enquiry here ashore they are assured is a signal from that officer to give warning to the French that a frigate is there and which side of the light she is on, that they may better avoid the danger of meeting with them".[5]

Due, no doubt, to their isolated situations lighthouses feature prominently in smuggling yarns and local legends as hiding places or clearing houses for contraband cargoes. In reality the situation was quite different. To a revenue man patrolling the coast in the bitter cold and dark of a winter's night, what could have seemed more inviting than the beckoning glow of a lighthouse? The prospect of a thorough warming before a cheery fire, an exchange of local gossip with the lightkeepers and the likelihood of a drop of something to keep out the cold, all or any of these were attractions too tempting to let go by. In consequence lighthouses drew revenue men like moths to a candle, and no self-respecting smuggler would care to be seen within miles of one.

A move to end the private ownership of lighthouses was foreshadowed in 1822, when a parliamentary committee was appointed to inquire into the state of foreign trade. Its terms of reference included an investigation into the revenue derived from lighthouses. In its report the Committee made some disparaging comments on the subject of privately owned lights. Of sixty-nine navigational lighthouses on the coasts of England and Wales, fourteen were in private hands and were yielding to their owners almost as much revenue as Trinity House was receiving from the other fifty-five. The report concluded with a particularly significant recommendation:

"Impressed with an opinion that much advantage would arise from the lights being generally placed under the Trinity House, Your Committee feel it incumbent upon them to suggest in such an event that on expiration of the terms, the patents in question, instead of being renewed to individuals, should be transferred to the Corporation."[6]

It was a logical and highly commendable suggestion, but as matters stood it was unachievable. Of those lights still in private hands the majority were secure for a great many years to come. A few, such as Tynemouth and Spurn Point, were held in perpetuity. The next twelve years saw the termination of only four of the fourteen remaining leases and in 1834 it was realised that there was no prospect of another falling vacant in the foreseeable future. The time was clearly ripe for government legislation, which came in the form of an Act of Parliament passed in 1836 empowering Trinity House to acquire by compulsory purchase all outstanding private leases. Included among these were four on the coast of East Anglia, the lights of Winterton, Orford Ness, Hunstanton and Harwich. They represented four of the oldest lighthouses in Britain, being among the first stations to be established and the last to continue in the hands of private owners. On 1st January, 1837, they passed into the care of Trinity House, to be added to those of Cromer and Lowestoft, already owned by the Corporation.

This book tells the story of these lights of East Anglia, and gives some account of the men and the families who owned them.

It would be encouraging to find that this was a story of compassion and genuine concern for the preservation of human life. Regrettably it is nothing of the kind. These were no examples of kindly lights, erected in a spirit of benevolence. They were business ventures, in the hardest and coldest sense of the term. Theirs is more a story of callousness and petty jealousies, of selfish motives indulged at the expense of humanitarian considerations. It is, moreover, a story which reveals some famous names from history in a none-too-favourable light.

Nevertheless, it is a true story, and one which deserves to be told, for it contributes much to local records and to the maritime history of this country.

CHAPTER ONE

Cromer

"It was three months and over,
Since the dear lad had started,
On the green downs at Cromer,
I sat to see the view,
On an open space of herbage,
Where the ling and fern had parted,
Betwixt the tall white lighthouse towers,
The old and the new."
(*Requiescat in pace*).

S INCE Jean Ingelow wrote those lines, the old has vanished from the scene and the hand of time has mellowed the new. For more than thirty years the white lighthouse towers kept each other company on Cromer cliffs, one doomed to destruction as yearly more land was lost to the sea, the other newly-built to take its place. The final reckoning came in December, 1866, when the old tower disappeared over the cliff, leaving its young apprentice to carry on the trade.

That kind of story occurs all too often along the twenty-five fragmentary miles that form this projecting shoulder of Norfolk. Geologically these cliffs are ill-equipped to withstand the full tidal assault of the North Sea. Their composition varies from fine light sand to heavy blue clay, all of which is readily eroded by the waves. The inevitable result is a long, sad story of lands lost to the sea, of entire villages that no longer exist, of estuaries silted up and headlands smoothed away.

Contrary to popular belief, the sea itself is not directly to blame for this receding coastline. When clay reaches saturation point it turns to slime and becomes a moveable mass; when excessively dry it shrinks and is interspersed with deep crevices which act as convenient waterways. That is why the most serious cliff-falls invariably follow periods of heavy rain, as the water accumulated underground finds its way down to the coast and literally bursts the cliffs apart. The function of the sea is to carry away the spoils, and this it can do with incredible speed. Except for a few fragments of the foundations, no trace of the old lighthouse was ever seen again.

Opposite: Cromer lighthouse, built by
Trinity House in 1832 to a design unlike that
of any other on the east coast of England.

At the time of the Domesday survey, Cromer did not rank as a town in its own right but formed part of the manor of Shipden. This township stood on the sea coast, about three miles to the northward, while immediately to the east the coastline projected into the sea to form a bold headland known as Foulness. Over the next three hundred years Shipden was gradually eaten away, and by the time Richard II came to the throne in 1377 it had been abandoned. It took the sea just thirty years to finish off the remains.

This large bite made Foulness an even more pronounced headland, fringed on three sides by cliffs sheer to the sea and crowned by some of the highest land in the district. In 1549 it was declared a beacon site, taking its light from the neighbouring beacon at Weybourne and passing the warning direct to the City of Norwich, whose beacon was placed on the church tower of St Giles-on-the-Hill.*

Like many other prominent features along this coast, Foulness has been completely washed away, and the modern Ordnance Survey map reveals a smooth and rounded coast where the headland once stood. Much of this erosion occurred during the nineteenth century. The year 1825 alone saw the fall of more than twelve acres along a front of three hundred yards. It seems very probable that the landslide of December, 1866, which carried away the old Cromer lighthouse, took with it the last remnants of Foulness and pruned the headland back to the general line of the coast. It is only by the expenditure of continuous human effort and enormous sums of money in the work of coast defence that Cromer itself has been saved from a fate similar to that of Shipden and Foulness.

*   *   *   *   *   *

In their journeys southward from the Tyne, the collier fleets kept close by the shore for as long as they possibly could, making use of conspicuous landmarks by which to navigate and keeping to the calmer waters between the shore and the outlying sands. The one section where this was not possible was the long haul between Flamborough Head and Yarmouth Roads. For this leg of the journey vessels were forced to stretch away towards the open sea, with all land lost to view as they followed a south-easterly course to carry them clear of the East Anglian coastal bulge. At the end of it all there came the necessity of making a fresh landfall as they approached the Norfolk coast, and that landfall had to be precisely right. Here, if anywhere, a guiding light was needed so that ships might know their position from as far as possible out to sea. The cliffs in the vicinity of Cromer offered the ideal site for such a light to be located, so it was inevitable that sooner or later an attempt would be made to establish a lighthouse here.

*The fire-basket has been preserved and is still displayed in this church.

Tradition tells of a light displayed in early times from the tower of Cromer church, and a tiny window high in the tower is claimed to have been intended for this purpose. If so, it could have served only local needs. The only light possible from such a small aperture would have been that of a candle, and although this might have given the town's fishermen a welcome mark to steer for, it would never have been visible far enough to be of benefit to ships still many miles out to sea. The call here was not for a feeble light of limited range but for a major navigational beacon, displayed from the highest practical elevation and visible to the furthermost point of the horizon.

In 1684 Captain Greenville Collins produced his chart of this coast, with relevant silhouettes and sailing directions. On a peak of cliff high above Cromer he depicted the tower of a lighthouse and added the comment: "Foulness which is high land on which standeth a Lighthouse, but no Fire kept in as yet."[1] Nor would there ever be, if Greenville Collins had only known. This tower, ruinous and abandoned, stood for many years on the cliffs at Foulness, a monument to the frustrated ambitions of a seventeenth-century speculator by the name of John Clayton.

It seems remarkable that such a man as John Clayton should have passed through this world and left behind such scant evidence that he ever existed. His name crops up from time to time in various state papers, sometimes as the recipient of a special grant or favour from King Charles II, more often as the central figure in some hotly-disputed speculative project. All this tells us nothing about him, apart from pointing to the fact that he must have been one of the most prominent and controversial figures of his day.

John Clayton lived at Parsons Green in Middlesex, a small Thames-side community standing at the point where two roads converged on their way to the river crossing at Putney. Today Parsons Green has become a suburb of Fulham with its own tube station on the District Line, but in John Clayton's time it was a distinct and highly select quarter, inhabited by "Gentry and persons of Qualitie."[2] As the name suggests, it began as an open space of greenery, offering common grazing rights and providing the site each year for a popular and widely renowned fair. Altogether it was a most pleasant and peaceful spot in which to live, with its houses grouped around the green, its meadows sloping down to the river and, for a few days each year, the excitement and pageantry of the fair.

Among the persons of quality who came to live here was Sir Jasper Clayton, merchant and shipowner, following his marriage to Mary, daughter of William Thompson of Tynemouth Castle. John Clayton was the son and heir of this marriage, and there was also a daughter, Rebecca.[3]

John Clayton first emerges from obscurity in November, 1664, when he was knighted by Charles II. We know nothing of his fortunes up to this time, nor of the reasons that brought him the honour of a knighthood. What we do know for certain is that he was a speculator, hot-headed, over-ambitious and not very scrupulous. His eye was for ever on the main chance, with the added advantage that he always had King Charles II to support him and further his cause.

Of all Sir John Clayton's aspirations, the one that caused the most controversy was his almost obsessive desire to own a lighthouse, or to be more exact, a whole chain of lighthouses. For more than seventeen years in pursuit of this ambition Clayton fought tooth and claw with the Brethren of the Trinity House, and he came at one stage within an ace of winning.

It all began in 1669, when Clayton, in association with one George Blake, submitted a petition to Charles II for permission to establish no fewer than four lighthouses at points along the east coast. These were to be at Flamborough Head on the coast of Yorkshire, on the Farne Islands, off Northumberland, in the St Nicholas Gat opposite Corton in Suffolk, and at Foulness Point near Cromer.

Despite the fact that little is known about Sir John Clayton, we can at least say with certainty that he was no seaman. Yet the various locations he proposed for his lighthouses had clearly been chosen with care. They represented four of the most salient and treacherous points on the entire east coast of England. It is a significant fact that at three of these places lighthouses were ultimately established and remain in service to this day, which is a clear indication that Clayton must have been advised by someone well in a position

Parson's Green, Middlesex, the birthplace and home of Sir John Clayton, as it is today.

to know. So it hardly comes as a surprise to learn that his partner, George Blake, who was rated for a house next to Clayton's at Parsons Green, was a shipmaster retired from the coasting trade.

It was the strict practice of Trinity House to oppose all attempts by private persons to establish lighthouses, on the grounds that it violated their own ancient rights. This frequently resulted in delays lasting several years before all the objections could be resolved and Letters Patent issued. The petition by Sir John Clayton and George Blake followed this typical course. Their proposal brought strong objections from Trinity House who declared that there was no further need of lights anywhere on the coasts of England. These protests had little effect, however, and following the recommendations of the Lords of the Treasury a Royal Warrant was issued on 22nd August, 1669:

> "To Sir John Clayton and George Blake for 60 years to build and maintain lighthouses on the northern coasts of England viz: St Nicholas Gat, Foulness, Flamborough Head and the Ferne Islands on a rent of £20 per annum, they receiving 1½d per ton from loaden ships and 1d from unloaden ones. Subject to them obtaining 500 Shipmasters signatures as to convenience and willingness to pay."[4]

The Letters Patent of Charles II followed on 25th October, and that would normally have clinched the matter. In the event it provoked the Trinity Brethren into mounting the most vigorous and prolonged campaign they had ever conducted against a private patentee, an ambiguous phrase in the wording of the grant being immediately seized on as grounds for further objections.

Meanwhile Clayton and Blake, cock-a-hoop over their success, publicly offered to provide a lighthouse free of all tolls on Spurn Point in the mouth of the Humber as a gesture of goodwill. On December 29th, 1669, a Royal Warrant was issued in their favour. The opposition by Trinity House did not result in the grant being nullified, but it did cause serious delays to Clayton's plans. Three years passed by, at the end of which time he had acquired sites for only two of his proposed lighthouses, at Corton and Flamborough Head. Elsewhere matters were less straightforward. Farne Island, for instance, was ecclesiastical land and was not readily available for a speculative venture such as this. But Charles II, who had been keeping a watchful eye on developments, was as always ready to come to Clayton's support. On 1st December, 1673, His Majesty addressed a letter to the Dean and Chapter of Durham:

> "In order to prevent in future the many wrecks which happen on the northern coasts of the kingdom, His Majesty has granted licence to Sir John Clayton and George Blake to erect certain lighthouses on the coast, one of which is to be on Ferne Island and understanding that the island

13

belongs to the Church of Durham and that the lease thereof is just expiring, he requests them on granting a new lease to reserve an acre of land for erecting a lighthouse with a highway to it at such rate as they think reasonable."[5]

Clayton now turned his attention to Foulness. Although this promontory was always regarded as an integral part of Cromer, it stood in fact within the boundaries of the neighbouring parish of Overstrand, as the present Cromer lighthouse still does today. The manor of Overstrand was first given to one Hugh de Reynes by Edward I in the late thirteenth century. With it went the right to claim wreck of the sea along this particular stretch of coast. It was to a descendant of this family, William Reynes, that Clayton made his approach. As a result, on 26th March, 1674, an agreement was signed between them under which Sir John Clayton "in consideration of a sum of thirty-five pounds of good, lawful English money" received from William Reynes a lease for sixty years of a parcel of land to the north of the footpath along the cliff-top "for the purpose of erecting a Lighthouse for the benefit of Navigation."[6] Since in the late summer of 1676 Clayton informed Charles II that his lighthouses were all built, we may assume that this tower on Foulness was about two years in the building.

Meanwhile, Trinity House was becoming more perturbed over this serious challenge to its monopoly. Further objections were lodged against the activities of Clayton and Blake, alleging that their lighthouses would be more of a hindrance than a help, and protesting that the signatures collected by Clayton were not those of qualified seamen.[7] As a result of these renewed objections Charles II commanded that the matter be referred to the Committee for Trade and Plantations for a full examination.

In early December, 1674, Sir John Clayton put his case to the Committee. He reminded them that he had already submitted the testimonial of several Masters and Pilots of experience and could, if required, have obtained the subscription of many hundreds more. The opposition to his proposed lights was due to the great influence which the Trinity House of London exerted over the other subsidiary Trinity Houses. Many shipmasters were members of these subsidiaries and were duty-bound to adhere to their official policy. There were, Clayton declared, some members of the London Trinity House who were now opposed to him although they had originally been in favour of his proposition. Clayton went on to suggest to the Committee that it should examine the results of an offshore survey that the Trinity Brethren had undertaken earlier that year. If, after inspecting this evidence, any of his proposed lights appeared to be less needful than the rest, then he would submit himself to His Majesty's pleasure therein. Furthermore, if the profits from any of the lights was found to be excessive then Clayton agreed to contribute to any work of charity carried out by Trinity House.

14

Sir John Clayton's lighthouse on Flamborough Head. Constructed of chalk with string courses of red brick, it is still standing three hundred years after erection.

It all sounded so open and above board. It was typical of the image that would-be lighthouse proprietors always tried to project, that of selfless and public-spirited citizens whose only concern was for the benefit of navigation, and to whom the prospect of personal gain was of no consequence whatever. But Clayton's case made no attempt to deny the accusation that he had presented a collection of dubious signatures in support of his claim, nor did it admit that the allegation had been the cause of many of his former supporters becoming disillusioned and changing their minds.

Early in 1675 the Trinity House of London circulated a letter to the other Trinity Houses asking them to state their opinions of Clayton's proposals, the replies being passed on to the Committee for Trade as evidence in the case against Clayton. The Trinity House of Newcastle considered that "the lights would be altogether unnecessary and would discourage the Coal Trade by lying heavily on it," while Hull Trinity House expressed the hope "that all lovers of Navigation will oppose Sir John Clayton's endeavours for Lighthouses. They would discourage shipbuilders and merchants by lessening their profits. They would be harmful and not useful." The Trinity House of Dover thought that "the said Lights would be unuseful and dangerous because ships might be lost by mistaking the lights."

Before any verdict was forthcoming from the Committee, Clayton succeeded in bringing his lighthouse at St Nicholas Gat into use. It was located at Corton, between Yarmouth and Lowestoft, and shone for the first time on the night of 22nd September, 1675. From the moment when it was first lit Corton Light brought problems for Clayton. To begin with there was some uncertainty as to the precise rate of tolls he was entitled to charge for this light. Matters were made all the more difficult when the Trinity Brethren began actively to discourage shipmasters from paying any dues for it at all.

A year later Clayton was no nearer bringing any of his other lights into service. Once again he was obliged to appeal to the King, explaining that although the lighthouses granted to himself and George Blake were all built, only the one at St Nicholas Gat was in commission owing to the legal objections that were continually being raised. Clayton therefore prayed that His Majesty would allow him to surrender his grant and would favour him instead with a patent for Corton alone. Charles II readily gave his consent, renewing the Corton grant under Letters Patent dated 23rd January, 1677.

Exactly how the Trinity Brethren reacted to this move, ultimately forcing Clayton to abandon his project altogether, is a story more directly concerned with Lowestoft that will be recounted in detail in that chapter. So far as Cromer and the other locations are concerned, the surrender of his original grant terminated Clayton's association with these places. For many years afterwards his tower stood on the cliffs at Foulness, useful no doubt as a daymark but destined never to show a light. It eventually disappeared in a fall of cliff about the year 1700. Only one of Clayton's five towers still survives, although it has never served in its intended capacity. It stands on Flamborough Head, close to the present lighthouse, a stark column of chalk commemorating twenty years of legal wrangling in the fight between Trinity House and private enterprise.

*   *   *   *   *   *

The crushing defeat of Sir John Clayton openly demonstrated that crossing swords with Trinity House could prove a costly, if not ruinous, undertaking, so it is not to be wondered at that nearly forty years went by before another serious attempt was made to place a light on Cromer cliffs. Several appeals were made to Trinity House during this time drawing attention to the pressing need for a light at this point on the coast, but the Corporation seemed disinclined to take any action in the matter. In 1718, however, a private promoter took the initiative by raising a petition on his own behalf. He was a merchant and prominent citizen of Ipswich by the name of Edward Bowell.

The petition came before a meeting of the Trinity House Court on 3rd December, 1718:

"A proposal was read from Edward Bowell of Ipswich for erecting a lighthouse at Foulness near Cromer, as was also a Subscription of a great number of Masters of Ships using the Coal Trade and along that coast, offering to pay ¼d per ton or ½d per Chaldron toward the Charge of erecting such a light.

"The proposal was adjourned to a later Court while the Clerk wrote to Newcastle, Yarmouth and other ports for their opinion as to the usefulness of such a light and the charges proposed for the maintenance thereof."[8]

Standing at the head of the Orwell estuary, the port of Ipswich is set back from the sea and lies remote from the coastwise shipping lanes. Somehow it is not the first place that springs to mind at the mention of east coast ports, but this is all rather deceptive, for it belies the importance and the prominence of the role played by Ipswich in the conduct of the collier trade. Here lived a community of merchants as numerous and opulent as any in London itself. Here on the banks of the Orwell were laid down some of the swiftest and sturdiest collier vessels ever built. And here too lived many of their masters, whiling away the long winter months between Michaelmas and Lady Day, traditionally the close season for the shipment of coal by sea.

In short, Ipswich was the focal point of the trade and its voice was the voice of the trade as a whole, which may, perhaps, go some way towards explaining why this petition from Edward Bowell received careful and serious consideration when all others had been curtly dismissed out of hand.

Edward Bowell, Portman and twice Bailiff of Ipswich,[9] was born in 1680 and lived all his life in the parish of St Clement's in Ipswich. He became a leading and highly respected figure, both in the commercial life of the port and in the municipal life of the town. Despite this, there is precious little to commemorate him in Ipswich today, so it becomes necessary to turn to Somerset House to piece together a picture of his background and circumstances from his will which he signed and dated on 6th August, 1737.[10]

One fact becomes quickly and firmly established; Edward Bowell was a man of substance. The house in which he lived, with its tenements, stables, coach-houses and yards, was one among several owned by him in the heart of Ipswich. A similar property stood in New Street, while another, in Fore Street, boasted the additional facility of a waterfront warehouse and quay. Edward Bowell was the owner, or part-owner, of at least three vessels trading out of Ipswich and he held a major share in a scheme to bring piped water to St Clement's parish. Further afield he owned farms and lands in the villages of Westerfield, Badingham and Trimley, with a watermill at Stowmarket and another in the nearby village of Combs.

At the time of the will, several members of the Bowell family were living in Ipswich, all in property owned by Edward Bowell, who clearly regarded himself as the father-figure of the family. There is no mention of him ever having had a wife, and it is a relation through marriage rather than a blood relative who emerges as the chief beneficiary.

This much can be gleaned from the last will and testament of Edward Bowell, landowner, farmer, merchant and miller, a man who, with due justification, described himself as "Gentleman".

It is a fair assessment of the esteem in which the port of Ipswich held him that his bid to set up a lighthouse at Foulness received the backing of virtually every master mariner and merchant in the port. It was not until the following April that the business again featured on the agenda of the Trinity House Court in London:

> "The several letters from Newcastle and Yarmouth being read in answer to those which had been wrote attesting to the usefulness and the reasonableness of the proposed duty.
>
> "It was resolved that if the said Edward Bowell were content to pay the Corporation the rent of one hundred pounds per annum and would at his own charge erect and constantly maintain the proposed lighthouse he may then apply in the name of the Trinity House for a Patent and the Corporation would grant him a lease for a term of 61 years commencing from the date of first kindling."[11]

St Clement's Church, Ipswich, once regarded as the seamen's church of the port. Edward Bowell was buried by the south-east doorway in October, 1737.

18

This was a tactic which the Trinity Brethren had used before. It was an astute and convenient way of satisfying the call for a lighthouse without involving themselves in the expense of actually providing it, yet at the same time not relinquising control of the situation, for when the lease had run its course they would be able to claim it back for themselves or farm it out for a further term as they thought fit. It will be seen in a later chapter that in the case of two of the earliest stations of all, at Caister and Lowestoft, the patent was granted initially to Trinity House and leased out to a private speculator.

One fact that went unmentioned in the foregoing minutes was that Edward Bowell would not reap the sole benefit from the lighthouse. He had entered into an equal partnership with one Nathaniel Life, owner of the ground on which the new tower was to be built, part of the land formerly leased by William Reynes to Sir John Clayton. It was Nathaniel Life, a member of the Life family of Marlingford near Norwich, who now claimed a half-share in Edward Bowell's project. It should be emphasised that Nathaniel Life and his successors played a very passive role in the building and management of the lighthouse, for it was Edward Bowell's idea, he was the motivating force, and all dealings with Trinity House were conducted in his name. Nevertheless, it is beyond doubt that Nathaniel Life did lay claim to half the proceeds; indeed, Edward Bowell refers in his will to his moiety share in the light at Foulness.

Once the Trinity Brethren's offer of a lease had been accepted by Bowell, the grant of a patent became a matter of mere formality. The Letters Patent of George I were issued on 9th September, 1719. Meanwhile, work on the lighthouse was all but complete. It was a straightforward structure of brick, octagonal in shape and of three storeys in height, designed to display the light from a coal fire burning in a wrought-iron basket or grate.

Less than three weeks after the Letters Patent were issued, there fell the convenient date of September 29th and on this Michaelmas Day Edward Bowell kindled his light for the first time. His lease from Trinity House was therefore valid until Michaelmas Day, 1780.

Edward Bowell's tower appears on several prints and engravings, but unfortunately none of them were made early enough, or from a view-point close enough, to provide a detailed illustration of the lighthouse in its original form. A dependable source of written information is found in the work of John Whormby, Clerk of the Trinity House between the years 1729 and 1744. Whormby's association with the Corporation began in 1711 when he became collector of its light dues at the Customs House in London, in which capacity he took a keen interest in the origin of the various lights and the patents under which their dues were levied. In 1729 he became Clerk of Trinity House, an appointment that enabled him to indulge his interest to a greater degree among the Corporation's archives. From the information he found there,

Whormby compiled a potted history of every lighthouse then in existence. The work, which was completed in 1746, was eventually published in 1861. Today John Whormby's accounts survive, while the original records from which they were composed are lost for all time due to the fact that a succession of disastrous fires has robbed Trinity House of much of its recorded history. The first was the Great Fire of London in 1666, to be followed in 1714 by another at the Corporation's premises then located in Water Lane. In more recent times much of the material that had survived the two previous incidents was lost in the great fire raid on London on the night of 29th-30th December, 1940. Consequently John Whormby's accounts may be regarded as the most authoritative and reliable source of reference in matters relating to Trinity House and the early development of lights and seamarks.

It is thanks to Whormby that we know the precise day when Edward Bowell first kindled his light at Foulness, and he also volunteers the information that this was "a close coal light", that is to say the fire was enclosed within a glazed lantern as opposed to an open and exposed brazier in which the fire was lulled to a heap of smouldering embers or was stimulated to white-hot intensity depending on the mood of the weather.

Nathaniel Life died in 1727, bequeathing the parcel of ground on which the lighthouse stood, and the half-share in the profits that went with it, to his son and heir, Philip Life. Ten years later, on 3rd October, 1737, Edward Bowell died, with forty-three years of the lease still unexpired. Under his will, proved in London during December of that year, the bulk of his estate was left to his housekeeper, Elizabeth Bowell. Elizabeth had married into the family but had been left a widow and had come to keep house for Edward. There is no clue as to the identity of her late husband, or of her precise relationship to Edward Bowell. All his properties in Ipswich, including the house in which he lived together with his interests in the piped water scheme and his farms and watermills in the surrounding countryside were left to Elizabeth subject to one overriding condition, "for so long time only as she shall continue a Widow and no longer."

The lighthouse itself was not included. Instead it passed to a nephew, Thomas Bowell, subject to the payment of certain annuities to sundry persons specified in the will, including one of twenty pounds to Elizabeth. At the time of his uncle's death Thomas Bowell was still a minor, so under the terms of the will the three executors undertook the guardianship of his interests in so far as his legacy was concerned. These executors were Henry Bowell, cousin to Edward, Samuel Parker of St Clement's Parish, Ipswich, and John Burkitt of Sudbury. To these three now fell the administrative tasks connected with the lighthouse. Theirs was the duty of ensuring that the disbursements were met and theirs was the responsibility of seeing that the half-portion due to Philip

Life was paid and that the several annuities as laid down in the will were duly paid from the portion remaining to Thomas Bowell.

Edward Bowell had one more request to make:

"And it is my Will and Pleasure that my Executors do give me decent Buryall and Erect over me a Tomb Stone in such manner as they and the said Elizabeth Bowell shall think fit."

This they did. On the stone they recorded his name together with the fact that he had twice held office as Bailiff of Ipswich. Additionally, by way of an epitaph, they made mention of his other notable achievement:

"He erected the Light at Foulness in Norfolk. Anno 1719."

This stone, which stood near the south-eastern entrance to Saint Clement's Church, has long since disappeared. As far back as 1830 it was described as being "much decayed." Most of the gravestones in this churchyard were

Cromer from the West Cliff showing Edward Bowell's lighthouse on the cliff edge, from a print published in 1798.

recently taken up and laid flat to form the paving slabs of a pedestrian precinct round the church.

The new owner of the lighthouse, Thomas Bowell, grew up in the family tradition of merchant and shipowner. In 1755 he was elected to serve as Bailiff of Ipswich as his father, uncle and grandfather had been before him. Throughout his ownership the light at Foulness was continued in its original form. There was no guarantee that Trinity House would renew the lease on its termination in 1780, consequently the further the term became expended the more slender grew the chance of any improvements being introduced. In the event the Trinity Brethren did agree to an extension of forty-two years terminating in 1822.

Meanwhile the ownership of the site devolved from Philip Life to his son, Caesar Life, on whose untimely death in 1763 it passed to an aunt, Mary Rant of Ipswich.

On the night of 31st October, 1789, a severe storm took heavy toll of ships and lives along the whole coast of East Anglia, prompting the Trinity Brethren to press for improvements to all the local lights. The resulting changes were more directly concerned with Winterton and will be described in more detail in that chapter, but so far as Cromer is concerned the incident heralded the end of the coal fire in favour of oil lighting. This form of illumination had been introduced at Hunstanton nearly twelve years previously, to be followed almost at once by Lowestoft.

Work was now put in hand to bring Cromer up to date, but the improvements here were not confined merely to a change of illuminant. A new form of equipment was designed consisting of a three-sided metal grid or frame which could be made to rotate under the pull of a descending weight. To each of the three sides was fixed a cluster of five oil lamps backed by silver-plated reflectors thirty-six inches in diameter. The whole assembly turned at the rate of one revolution in three minutes, so that when seen from a distance the effect was that of a single clear-cut flash every minute as each face of the frame in turn came into view.

The new light shone for the first time on the night of 8th September, 1792.[12] The conversion had taken almost three years, but now that it was completed Cromer could boast that it was one of only two lights in existence recognisable by an intermittent, self-identifying flash.[13]

When the lease came to an end exactly thirty years later Cromer was still one of the most powerful and efficient lights on the coasts of England. Ownership had by now become dispersed among the descendants of Thomas Bowell, but this time the Trinity Brethren declined to farm the lease out to private enterprise for a further period. During the final years of the term the clear profits varied from £2,819 in 1818 to £2,217 during the following year and £2,348 in 1820. In 1821 negotiations began for the outright purchase of the property by Trinity House, the figure finally agreed upon being £3,892. The lighthouse came under the Corporation's management for the first time on the night of 29th September, 1822.

During this period two young women were employed as lightkeepers, receiving from Trinity House the sum of £50 a year plus perquisites.[14] It was by no means usual for women keepers to be on the payroll and one wonders if they were perhaps widows of men who had lost their lives in the Trinity House service. The expectation of perquisites suggests that lighthouse visiting was as popular with society of the early nineteenth century as it is with that of the present day.

It was not long before the first signs of trouble to come became apparent. Year by year the crumbling remains of Foulness Point continued to fall into the sea. For most of the time this was a gradual though constant process, but every now and then a fall would occur on a massive and serious scale. One such occasion was on 15th January, 1825, when no less than twelve acres gave way along a three-hundred foot frontage on the seaward side of the lighthouse. On 19th August, 1832, a similar fall made it obvious that sooner or later the

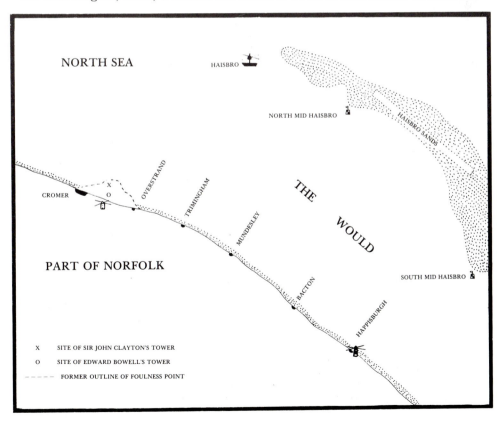

NORTH SEA

PART OF NORFOLK

X   SITE OF SIR JOHN CLAYTON'S TOWER
O   SITE OF EDWARD BOWELL'S TOWER
-----   FORMER OUTLINE OF FOULNESS POINT

The old and new lighthouses at Cromer, showing the new Trinity House tower of 1833 on the left and Edward Bowell's threatened lighthouse on the right.

lighthouse itself would be carried away. It was decided while there was still time to build a replacement tower and to abandon the existing one to its fate. Work now commenced on a new tower four hundred yards further back from the cliff edge. It was completed within a remarkably short space of time, emphasising the urgency of the situation, and came into service on the night of 29th June, 1833, exhibiting a light twice as powerful as before. The idea of the triple-sided frame was retained but the number of lamps was increased to ten on each face, making it necessary to reduce the diameter of the reflectors from three feet to twenty-one inches.

That tower has continued in service at Cromer to the present day. There are features of its design which lead one to wonder whether it was originally intended to stand here at all.

All the lighthouses on the east coast of England are shore stations. Some stand on cliff-top sites, some on shingle headlands, others even in the middle of seaside towns. Consequently they have no need of massive stone blocks for strength and durability, nor are their foundations keyed into the underlying rock to withstand the perpetual pounding of heavy seas. On this coast the sole need is for a tower of straightforward and simple design with the one object of giving elevation to the light. They need to be built of nothing stronger than red brick, and that brickwork needs to be no more intricate or specialised than would go into the building of the average factory chimney. It will be seen in the course of later chapters that in nearly all cases these towers were in fact the work of small firms of local jobbing builders.

By its construction and general proportions Cromer stands out as utterly alien to all other lighthouses between the Tyne and the Thames. The only brickwork is in the short section joining the base and the gallery. It is surrounded at lantern level by a heavy ballustrade rather than the light iron railings that suffice at other lighthouses. The gallery and lantern platform are of solid stone; a stone so hard that when Trinity House engineers came to fit a new lantern in 1958 they found to their surprise that their pneumatic drills could make hardly any impression upon it. No stone such as that ever came from beneath the soil of Norfolk. It had to be shipped here by sea and landed on the beach in the same way that coal and other commodities were.

Cromer was notorious for the difficulties attending the unloading of cargoes due to the long, steep haul up the face of the cliff to the town. Coal could only be taken up at the rate of half a chaldron, say about twenty-six hundred-weights, at a time and it took four horses all their strength to do it. Because of this the price of coal in Cromer was higher than at many places twenty miles inland.[15] But the lighthouse site was another hundred feet higher than the town, reached only by a narrow path which climbed tortuously to the uppermost peak of cliff. To this isolated and inaccessible vantage-point would have to be taken all the heavy and unwieldy material intended for the new lighthouse, so the question must inevitably be asked, why should the Trinity Brethren have gone to so much additional trouble and needless expense when they could have built a straightforward tower of locally-made brick at a fraction of the cost?

Only one explanation readily suggests itself; that the materials were already available, having been recovered from some tower that had been replaced at another point on the coast, or had been fashioned in readiness for the building of a new tower somewhere else. This possibility would go a long way towards resolving several questions to which there are otherwise no logical answers. It would explain, for instance, why Cromer lighthouse is of a design and general appearance more in keeping with lighthouses in the West Country or on the coasts of Wales. It would account for the figures "228 feet 10 inches" carved upon the door sill, when the true height of this particular spot is only 223 feet above sea level. Above all, it would explain the incredibly short time that it took for the work to be completed; ten months and ten days, precisely, from the time that the old tower was first threatened.

All this is, of course, mere conjecture, with little chance of it ever being proved or disproved. Unfortunately the incendiary raid in December, 1940, which caused such gaps in the London skyline left the Trinity House on Tower Hill a smouldering shell, with much of its recorded history lost in the flames. Somewhere among those archives could well have been a clue to the true origin

Left: Cromer lighthouse and the adjoining keepers' house in 1895.

Opposite: The same tower with new keepers' houses and the smaller lantern installed in 1958.

of Cromer lighthouse. Perhaps they included some books of account, or a set of plans, or even some details noted by the engineer-in-charge, Mr James Walker. All that can now be said for certain is that the situation which arose at Cromer in 1832 was regarded as being of the utmost urgency, calling for the lighthouse to be replaced with the minimum of delay. The tower which took its place would, to all outward appearances, have been the slowest, most toilsome and costly way imaginable of going about it.

In reality there was no urgency about the situation at all. Not that there was any way of knowing it at the time, but this latest fall of cliff was to be the last subsidence on a major scale for a good many years to come. The pattern of erosion now changed, or rather reverted, to a process of sustained attack along a broad front, instead of the occasional large bite taken at one specific point as had been the case during the past decade. These changed conditions earned a reprieve for the old lighthouse, enabling it to survive for more than thirty years. In 1841 the distance between it and the cliff-edge was reported to be 72 feet. It took just 25 years for those 24 yards to be eaten away.

Weather-wise, the autumn of 1866 was atrocious. Throughout the whole of November it hardly stopped raining at all. The low-lying areas inland of Yarmouth and in the Horsey-Hickling basin became drowned lands again, as they had been two thousand years before. As the month progressed the rain storms began to be reinforced by winds of gale force. On the last day of November the elements staged something of a grand finale. Hard on the heels

of a twelve-hour downpour came a thunderstorm accompanied by a minor hurricane. Nearly a dozen wrecks occurred along the stretch of coast between Cromer and Lowestoft, while on land there was extensive damage to property. At Yarmouth the wind demonstrated its strength most convincingly by lifting the town's gasometer bodily and heaving it over on to its side where it lay "like an enormous piece of crumpled brown paper."[16]

Such a prolonged period of abnormal rainfall invariably gives rise to a spate of erosion and the ultra-wet autumn of 1866 was no exception. Almost immediately a fall took place at Cromer which left the former lighthouse balanced on the extreme edge of a precipice, and within a few days a second and more extensive subsidence occurred. It happened during the morning of Friday, 7th December, when a cliff-mass of several acres came down with a noise like thunder. Several people walking on the beach had to run for their lives as hundreds of tons of spoil piled up against the foot of the cliffs. High above, an enormous bite, 130 yards across, had been taken out of the cliff top. On the beach the way was barred by a jumbled mass of gravel and clay projecting like a miniature headland into the sea. Somewhere underneath it lay the rubble of Edward Bowell's old lighthouse. News of the incident soon spread, but much to the disappointment of the many sightseers drawn to the spot, not so much as a brick of the old tower was to be seen.

Possibly on account of this the belief has always persisted that no trace of the lighthouse was ever seen again. However, the Norfolk historian, Walter

27

Rye, writing in 1888 observed that fragments of the foundations had been laid bare during that year by further scouring of the cliff.

This latest landslip had, within a matter of seconds, altered Cromer's familiar silhouette. The high peak of cliff eastwards of the town appeared strangely bare with only one of its twin towers left to dominate the skyline. It seemed equally unfamiliar by night with the new lighthouse no longer lighting up the ghostly image of its companion, as it had done for the past three decades.

In 1872 paraffin oil, or kerosene as it was generally known, became available in this country. The lamp oil in general use at this time was colza, which had in turn replaced whale oil. Colza was extracted from the seed of a turnip-like plant belonging to the brassica family and went by the alternative name of rape-seed oil. The plant is still grown as a crop in parts of this country, producing in due season fields of such vivid yellow that it is frequently mistaken for mustard.

Kerosene now promised to be cheaper, cleaner and altogether more efficient. Unfortunately it burned at a higher temperature and this fact alone precluded its use at Cromer. The excessive heat given off by thirty burners revolving in the confined space of the lantern had always created something of a problem. Cromer was, in fact, the most extravagant station in service in

terms of oil consumption. It burned about 970 gallons of best colza oil yearly, more than three gallons each night during the darkest months of the winter. Despite these disadvantages colza oil remained in use at Cromer until the advent of coal gas made it possible to improve the efficiency of the light with no increase in the amount of heat generated in the lantern.

Domestic gas first came to Cromer in 1875, when the town's gasworks was completed. Ten years later all the main streets were gas lit. By the turn of the century the new illuminant was being adopted at those lighthouses situated conveniently close to a source of supply. In 1905 a spur was taken off the main in Overstrand Road and led up the steep incline to the lighthouse.

So great was the luminosity of town gas compared with that of colza oil that it proved possible to increase the light from its existing 36,000 candlepower to 49,000 candlepower using only seven burners on each face of a two-sided frame, instead of the ten on each side of a triple-faced frame as previously. The old frame was now replaced by a single upright assembly on which the fourteen lamps and reflectors were fixed back to back in two groups of seven. This apparatus turned at the rate of one complete revolution each minute, so producing a flash of light every thirty seconds.

The system of boosting light rays by placing reflectors behind the light-source, technically known as catoptric lighting, was already outdated.

Opposite: The Lighthouse Hills at Cromer seen across Happy Valley about 1910. The Links Hotel on the right was destroyed by fire in 1936.

Right: Viewed from almost the same direction in an engraving published by Rock and Company in 1867, when the lighthouse was the only building in the area.

Science had now brought to near-perfection the system known as dioptric lighting, which relied on optical prisms placed in front of the light to intensify the beams. This was initially a French invention dating from as early as 1822, but subsequent development by the Scottish lighthouse engineer, Alan Stevenson, and the Birmingham firm of Chance Brothers had now made this the ultimate in light projection. Nevertheless more than half a century was to pass before dioptric lighting came to Cromer.

In 1935 it was decided to connect the lighthouse to the electricity mains so that it would no longer be entirely dependent on domestic gas. For the next twenty-three years the light was produced by a combination of gas burners and electric lamps. Throughout the war years Cromer, together with most other coastwise lights, was lit only as and when Admiralty requirements dictated.

By 1958 this was the last English lighthouse still using the catoptric form of lighting. In June of that year the station was temporarily closed for modernisation, the entire lantern being removed and replaced by one containing a prismatic lens. It was this operation that revealed the ultra-hard nature of the stone with which the tower was built. The new equipment was far more compact than the old revolving frame, enabling the new lantern to be on a correspondingly smaller scale. After an interval of five months the lighthouse shone again on the night of 6th November, 1958. It was now an all-electric light combining the power of a hundred-thousand candles and switched on and off at source in a series of five flashes repeated at fifteen-second intervals.

So Cromer lighthouse was brought to its present state. In this age of automation it is the only lighthouse on the coast of East Anglia to be watched round the clock by a full complement of keepers. Its position on the cliffs gives it one of the highest elevations of any British lighthouse, the focus of the light being 274 feet above sea level, enabling it to be seen over a distance of twenty-three miles on a clear night.

The presence of Cromer lighthouse at this point where the Norfolk coast thrusts itself into the path of approaching ships is vital. In particular it benefits those vessels coming down from the north, assisting them to make their landfall safely and precisely, which is exactly what Sir John Clayton had in mind when he first proposed a lighthouse here more than three hundred years ago.

Cromer lighthouse in 1925.

CHAPTER TWO

Winterton

"But we made but slow way towards the shore, nor were we able to reach the shore until, being past the lighthouse at Winterton, the shore falls off to the west towards Cromer, so the land broke off a little the violence of the wind."

THE words are Robinson Crusoe's—or more precisely those of his creator, Daniel Defoe. Anyone reading the opening chapters of this famous story, with conditions off the Norfolk coast so vividly described and place-names specifically mentioned, might well conclude that the author was drawing on his personal knowledge of this locality. Such an assumption would be quite wrong. Defoe at this time knew only what he had heard and read.

Daniel Defoe was a man of many parts, shopkeeper, traveller, tax collector, journalist, owner of a brickworks, not to mention a proven bankrupt and therefore in law a criminal. Twice he found himself on the wrong side of Newgate's inhospitable doors. Above all he was an observer, and he observed not so much to satisfy his own curiosity as to pass his findings on to others. One suspects that Defoe derived more satisfaction from imparting information than from acquiring it in the first place. Eighteenth-century society, thrilled by the adventures of Robinson Crusoe and shocked by those of Moll Flanders, clamoured for his first-hand accounts and vivid descriptions.

In fact it was not until 1722, with *Robinson Crusoe* already written and published, that Daniel Defoe first came to Winterton and saw for himself the place whose evil reputation had prompted him to use it as a setting. He found conditions even worse than he had been led to expect. He found a village built almost entirely out of shipwreck, with sheds and barns, pig-sties and even garden fences built out of timber salvaged from wrecked ships. He found the whole stretch of coast littered with the remains of ships, their carcasses picked clean by the bands of local wreckers to whom all this was looked upon as "God's Grace." And Defoe found also that there was not just one Winterton lighthouse, but four:

"The dangers of this place being thus considered it is no wonder that upon this shore beyond Yarmouth there are no less than four lighthouses kept flaming every night besides the lights at Caister north of the town."

Defoe learned of the appalling toll taken by Winterton Ness, the great promontory of sand and dune which reached out into the sea to throw a barrier across the entrance to Yarmouth Roads. He was told of the disasters which had happened there, such as the day in 1554 when more than fifty ships foundered in a single day and the tragedy of 1692 when a thousand sailors perished in a single night.

When considering Winterton and its maritime history it is important to realise that Winterton Ness as it existed in the days of Daniel Defoe was vastly different from the shallow bulge which appears on an Ordnance Survey map of the present day. With the possible exception of Easton Ness, to the south of Lowestoft, the Ness at Winterton was the most salient point along the east coast. Understandably the sailors dreaded Winterton more than any other place between the Tyne and Thames.

It has always been held that Winterton lights were established under a grant made to Sir William Erskine and Sir John Meldrum. In fact this is not

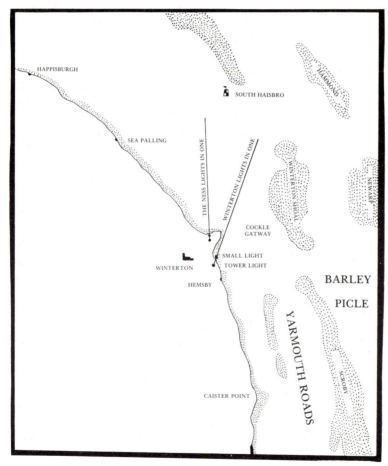

altogether correct. Although it was these two who ultimately received the patent, the original petition had been presented by, and granted in favour of, Sir William Erskine and a certain Dr Welwood. John Meldrum's interest was acquired later when he purchased Dr Welwood's share in the project. This is confirmed by Meldrum himself in a letter written several years later.

There was in fact a considerable delay between the presentation of the petition and the issuing of the Letters Patent, and it was during this time that John Meldrum secured Dr Welwood's share. The rapid growth of the trade in sea coals brought repeated pleas for lights at Winterton. In 1600 the Trinity Brethren carried out an extensive survey of Yarmouth Roads. As a result, two candle lighthouses were erected at Caister, a few miles down the coast, but no reason was found for any lights at Winterton. Caister lights have long disappeared from the scene, leaving little evidence that they ever existed. One reference to them still survives in the form of a letter addressed to a certain Mr Hill appointing him lightkeeper in 1628. He was instructed "to live at Caister in Norfolk, and to exhibit in either lighthouse three candles of three to the pound which are to be lighted immediately after sunset and continue them burning until fair day."

In 1609 a further survey prompted the Trinity Brethren to establish their lights at Lowestoft. Four years later a party of Elder Brethren surveyed all the sands and sounded all the channels in Yarmouth Roads. There was, they reported, "no cause to set up any lighthouse at Winterton."

But if the Trinity Brethren were loth to build a lighthouse here, others were only too anxious to do so, and in 1615 Sir William Erskine and Dr Welwood, with the backing of numerous merchants and masters engaged in the Newcastle trade, submitted a petition to James I. Despite his Scottish ancestry and upbringing, there was one characteristic in which James did not run true to form. He was far from wise in money matters. A compulsive spender, he lived for the most part beyond his means. His Coronation alone is reputed to have cost twenty thousand pounds, and his life since then had been one of perpetual spending and lavish entertaining. To his fellow countrymen who had followed him from Scotland, James' generosity knew no bounds. Gifts of money, grants of land and coveted titles were bestowed upon them and they had only to ask in order to receive almost any favour they cared to name. One of them was now asking for a lighthouse.

James had succeeded to the throne of Scotland at the age of eleven months on the abdication of his mother, Mary Queen of Scots. Responsibility for his safety and welfare had been entrusted to the Earl and Countess of Mar, and later to Sir Alexander Erskine. James had been raised and educated with Erskine's sons and they had become his boyhood companions. James, therefore, had much to thank the Erskines for, and they in turn could be numbered among his staunchest and most loyal supporters. For these reasons, then, any petition which bore the name of an Erskine stood every chance of success, and this case proved no exception. James readily assented, only to meet with insurmountable opposition on the part of Trinity House.

On coming to the English throne James had, as a matter of formality, renewed the Trinity House charter. He subsequently went further and signed an Order-in-Council declaring that the sole right to erect lights and seamarks was vested in the Trinity House of Deptford Strond. In an effort to foil the Winterton grant the Trinity Brethren now confronted James with this evidence. The setting up of lights and seamarks was, they protested, their own exclusive right, and they prayed that the King would not give that right away to others. They had a fifty-year-old Act of Parliament to prove their point, and furthermore had not James only recently put his name to a document confirming it? The facts were indisputable. James had unwittingly deprived himself of a substantial source of revenue. The Attorney General, Sir Francis Bacon, was called in to seek a solution but failed to find one, and matters came to a standstill.

Clearly the first round had gone in favour of the Trinity Brethren. By enforcing this state of legal deadlock they had ensured that Erskine and Welwood's grant would be held in abeyance and this had won for them a valuable respite. Meanwhile there was no reason why the Trinity Brethren should not exercise their own legal rights and erect a light themselves. Two Elder Brethren were issued with urgent instructions:

> "Make your undelayed repair to Winterton in the County of Norfolk and there consider of some fit place near Wintertonness where you may cause a turrett or watch-house to be erected for the burning and keeping of a light of sea coals to be maintained near the said Ness for the better conduction of ships and vessels coming out of the roads; also two other lighthouses for leading marks".[1]

The two Elder Brethren were, in all probability, Captain Cooke and Captain Geere, who are on record as having been directed to "go to Winterton and make lighthouses there".

Work commenced in March, 1616, and by the following June what was called the Tower Lighthouse had been completed near Winterton village at a cost of £600. It was provided free of tolls from then until the next April, when a rate of sixpence per twenty chaldrons of coal was introduced.

It is at this point that John Meldrum first comes into the story. By purchasing Dr Welwood's share of this frustrated concession, he embarked on the first of several lighthouse projects in which he was to become involved. John Meldrum's career in lighthouses came near to being as ambitious and audacious as that of Sir John Clayton, but with the difference that Meldrum's every venture turned out to be as successful as Clayton's proved abortive.

A view of the village of Winterton by A. M. and J. B. Ladbrooke, with the octagonal lighthouse built by Sir Edward Turnour in 1685 on the right. *Norfolk County Library*

There can be little doubt that had it not been for the determined intervention of Trinity House these two enterprising individuals would have monopolised the lighting of the whole east coast, with lighthouses at every salient point from the Farne Islands to the Forelands of Kent.

John Meldrum was first and foremost a soldier, whose service had already been sufficiently outstanding to have come to the notice of the King. In April, 1611, in reward for his services during the uprisings in Ireland, Meldrum received the grant of extensive estates in County Fermanagh. He went on to take part in the wars in the Low Countries, acquitting himself so well that he was knighted by James I at Windsor on 6th August, 1622. He was held in as high esteem by Charles I as he had been by James and in 1627, following an expedition to La Rochelle, Meldrum received the sum of £600 as a personal reward from the King. He was by this time an established favourite at Court and in 1635 received the grant of the patent for lights on the North and South Forelands. Almost simultaneously Meldrum secured an additional grant for lights at Orford Ness, making him the proprietor of a chain of coast lights reaching from Norfolk to Kent.

But for the young John Meldrum in this year 1616 all this lay far in the future. Captain John Meldrum, as he now was, an officer of some ten years' standing, needed to become much more influential at Court before he would risk being presumptuous enough to ask for a lighthouse as a reward for his years of loyal service. Perhaps it was this thought that persuaded Meldrum to gamble a large sum in purchasing Dr Welwood's share of a concession which, as likely as not, would never reach fruition. If the gamble paid off it would prove a short cut to the ownership of a lighthouse. Perhaps he reasoned that the question of patent grants for lights could not be left in abeyance for ever and that sooner or later a decision would have to come, a decision to humour the King if heads were not to roll.

It can be safely assumed that the geographical location was irrelevant. Winterton itself meant little or nothing to John Meldrum and the chances are that up to that time he had never been within a hundred miles of the place. One is tempted to say that he had never even heard of it before, but this could hardly be, for all the world had heard of Winterton and the grim happenings there on wild winter nights when ships were driven helpless before the wind.

Whatever his motives may have been, however, it proved a sound speculation on Meldrum's part, for within a short time Sir Henry Yelverton replaced Sir Francis Bacon as Attorney General. Unlike his predecessor, Yelverton refused to make heavy going of the issue of coast lights and quickly gave a ruling on the matter. He confirmed that the sole right to erect lights and seamarks belonged to Trinity House, but he found no reason in law why the Sovereign should not make additional grants to other persons should it please him to do so. As a legal decision it was a bit thin, nor did it even sound particularly convincing, but at least it gave James the loophole he needed and Henry Yelverton got off to a good start in his new office. By hook or by crook the problem had been resolved, to the satisfaction of all concerned, except of course the Trinity Brethren, who by this time were probably quite accustomed to being ridden over rough-shod.

The way was now open for the two would-be proprietors of Winterton lights to proceed with their project. Accordingly, under the Great Seal of England and signed at Westminster on 18th February, 1617, Sir William Erskine and his new partner received their patent, as the Trinity Brethren put it, "to the griefe and discouragement of all Merchants, Owners and Masters trading those northern coasts."[2] The Brethren retaliated by encouraging shipmasters to refuse payment of dues and offered to provide the lights themselves in return for the rate of sixpence per twenty chaldrons. Eventually Erskine and Meldrum lodged an appeal with the Privy Council, who ordered that a board of enquiry should be set up to look into the whole affair.

The dispute was heard before a special court convened in March, 1621, under the presidency of Lord Zouch, Lord Warden of the Cinque Ports. It was explained that although the action was brought in the names of Sir William Erskine and Mr John Meldrum,[3] thereafter referred to as the Patentees, in fact an agreement had lately been reached between the two plaintiffs and John Meldrum now held the sole interest.

The Patentees' grievance was that although Trinity House had held the right to establish lights and seamarks since the eighth year of Elizabeth's reign, in all that time they could never be persuaded to erect a light at Winterton, despite repeated requests to do so. But now that the Patentees had procured a grant and had established the lights so essential to navigation, at a cost to themselves of between £2,500 and £3,000, the Trinity Brethren were attempting to prevent the dues being paid. Furthermore the Trinity Brethren had declared that these tolls were excessive and were offering to provide the lights themselves at a rate of sixpence upon every twenty chaldrons of coal.

In their reply[4] to these allegations the Elder Brethren dealt first with the complaint that they had always in the past declined to erect any lights at Winterton. This, they admitted, was perfectly true; for the simple reason that up to now there had never been the need. About six years ago a party of Elder Brethren had been sent to conduct an offshore survey with instructions to set up as many seamarks as they thought fit, but no need had been found for any lighthouses at Winterton, so good was the channel there. But since then, in the course of one severe winter, the sands had suddenly altered and the channel had become dangerous, so that during a recent tempest that came by night some forty-five vessels had been lost. This disaster, the Brethren went on to relate, had been the deciding factor in persuading them to establish their "Tower Light" at Winterton, which they provided free of tolls from June until the following April. During this time the Patentees had been favoured with a grant from His Majesty and had commanded that the Trinity Brethren should extinguish their light. This request had been complied with, whereupon the Patentees had broken down the door of the Tower Light and kept their own lights in it until their towers were ready.

As to the claim that these towers cost between two-and-half and three thousand pounds, it was the Corporation's considered opinion that they could have been built for one hundred and fifty pounds. Of John Meldrum the Brethren would only say that he was no seaman and therefore could not possibly understand the nature of sands and the flowing of tides. But the Brethren themselves were all seamen, bred to the sea from childhood, and when it came to knowledge of marine affairs and the setting up of seamarks they were in their element. If this was not sufficient reason to prove them more qualified than anyone else to have charge of the lights then, they declared emphatically, "let us suffer and be hanged at the Gates of the King's Court for example to others."

The enquiry then heard the case put by John Meldrum.[5] He began by producing a set of accounts showing the amount collected from shipping at the Customs House in London in return for Winterton Lights. These showed that in the two years 1619 and 1620 the fire light at Winterton village and the two candle lights out on the Ness had earned between them a total of £766. A further set of figures estimated the annual cost of maintaining these three lights to be £350. The rate of one penny by the ton from passing ships was, Meldrum protested, wholly inadequate. From it he could expect an annual revenue of no more than £900, and what with the cost of purchasing Dr Welwood's share of the patent and later buying out Sir William Erskine's interest he already found himself "out of purse" to the extent of £3,600. This took no account of other charges that he might incur should the lighthouses have to be moved or rebuilt "according to the alterations of that shelfe." With such unattractive prospects one wonders why Meldrum wanted to retain the grant at all.

The offer by Trinity House to provide the lights in return for sixpence per twenty chaldrons was, in Meldrum's view, quite impracticable. And what an opportune time, he pointed out, for such an offer to be made. When the Patentees had suffered the expense of building the lighthouses and had brought them into service, only then had the Masters of Trinity House come forward with this offer; only then, when there was the prospect of some profit to be derived, had they taken an interest in the situation at Winterton. In fifty-five years they had not built a single lighthouse apart from Winterton Tower and that only as a means of foiling the Patentees' endeavours. It was really because they wanted to monopolise all for themselves and eliminate any risk of competition.

As to the accusation that he had forcibly entered the Tower Lighthouse, Meldrum declared that an agreement had been reached between the two sides that while the present matter remained in dispute the lights would be continued for the benefit of navigation. A light would be displayed from the Trinity Brethren's Tower Lighthouse with the costs being borne by the Patentees. But, Meldrum alleged, the Trinity Brethren had failed to honour this covenant, so he had been obliged to break down the door of the lighthouse and rekindle the light to avoid further shipwreck. As to the maintenance of the lights, nothing was necessary except to make a fire and light a few candles at a given time, and it needed no qualified seaman to perform a simple task such as that. Meldrum was at a loss to know why the Trinity Brethren placed such emphasis on the fact that he was not a qualified seaman. Sir Edward Howard, who had erected the lights at Dungeness and one Bushell, who had established those at Caister, were no seamen either, but they were not objected to; possibly, Meldrum pointed out accusingly, because they had each agreed to pay Trinity House a fee of £20 per year. Meldrum had no doubt that if he had made a similar offer he too would have been esteemed qualified.

So, with the proceedings having deteriorated to the level of something approaching a slanging match, the evidence for the two sides was completed. It must be conceded that John Meldrum had argued his case in a plausible fashion; striving throughout to preserve the image of a public benefactor, prompted solely by humanitarian motives. It was a strategy which stood him in good stead and proved convincing enough to sway the issue in his favour. His grant was confirmed and Trinity House was precluded from maintaining any lights within two miles of Winterton. For the next sixteen years the lights remained in Meldrum's hands, during which time they continued in the form of a single navigational beacon near Winterton village and a pair of leading lights on the Ness.

In 1634 Meldrum successfully petitioned for lights on Orford Ness and in April the following year was equally successful in acquiring lights on the North and South Forelands. Having established these two stations, he suddenly disposed of his Winterton and Orford grants to Alderman Gerard Gore of London, leaving himself in possession of the Foreland lights only. In 1637 Alderman Gore surrendered the remaining term of the Winterton lease, receiving in its place a new grant which incorporated Winterton and Orford into one holding. This lease was for a term of fifty years, expiring in 1687, at an annual rent of twenty pounds. In return a rate of tolls was fixed to cover both sets of lights, an arrangement which was to persist throughout the remaining two hundred years that the lights were in private ownership.

The history of these two stations thus becomes inseparably bound together; from now on to speak of Winterton is automatically to speak of Orford Ness in so far as private owners and their leases are concerned. The remainder of this account, therefore, will concern itself mainly with the activities of Trinity House at Winterton. The various private persons who come into the story will receive only casual mention in passing but will feature in greater detail in the chapter devoted to Orford Ness.

Before many years had passed, the Trinity Brethren were presented with another chance to establish themselves at Winterton. Soon after 1670 a series of storms caused drastic scouring of the coast and an upheaval of the outlying sands. By 1677 a completely new channel had formed close inshore, offering a deeper and more direct entry into Yarmouth Roads. In August of that year a petition was presented at Trinity House calling for an additional small lighthouse to be erected on the foreshore,[6] to serve as a front light to the existing Tower Light and to be sited in such a way that the two lights in line would indicate a safe approach to the new channel. The petition was debated at a Trinity House Court held on August 25th. It was resolved that the Corporation should approach the Duke of York who, as Lord High Admiral, was a member of the Privy Council, and seek his support in obtaining a grant for the new lighthouse from the King.[7] The minutes of the next Court held the following week record the favourable outcome:

> "That this Corporation having yesterday waited on His Majesty for his lease, his Royal Highness interposing in favour of the same, being addressed to about it on Tuesday last for directing a new candle lighthouse at Winterton Ness for a longshore mark placed with the Great Lighthouse there.
>
> RESOLVED: That Captain Till and Mr Bayley be writ to, to go about erecting a more substantial boarded lighthouse at Winterton Ness to be soe placed alongs't mark for the inner new channel to be made to remove about as doth Leystaff."[8]

Captain Hugh Till and Mr Simon Bayley were both Elder Brothers of Trinity House and were responsible for supervising the building of several of the Corporation's lighthouses about this time. Their names are still to be seen carved above the door lintel of the old St Agnes lighthouse on the Scilly Isles.

The patent for the new light authorised Trinity House to levy dues at the rate of sixpence a ship of one hundred tons or less and two shillings for all vessels above. The grant was operative as from Michaelmas Day, 1677. So there now existed at Winterton this unique arrangement of a low light administered by Trinity House answering to a high light in the ownership of a private proprietor. Dues were levied as if for two separate lighthouses, the respective parties being responsible for collecting their own tolls.

Unfortunately the Trinity Brethren's new light was introduced at the commencement of what proved to be a prolonged phase of coastal erosion. Early in 1683 the keeper of the Small Light sent word to London that the sea had encroached to a point where the lighthouse was in danger of being washed away. Now it so happened that one of the Corporation's senior members lived at nearby Somerleyton, in the vicinity of Lowestoft. He was Sir Thomas Allin, prominent Lowestoft merchant, Elder Brother of Trinity House and one of its eight appointed Assistants. The Clerk of Trinity House despatched the following letter to him dated 17th February 1683:

> Honourable Sir,
> Here inclosed is a copy of a letter from Mr Clement Trotter who looks after the small Light at Winterton which informed this Corporation of the dangerous Condition that Lighthouse is in, by reason of the breaking in of the Sea there; which I am commanded to communicate to Your

Honour, that Your Honour, if it may Suite with your Affaires, and if the season be not inconsistant with the tenderness of your years, may upon a view take Such Care for the Security thereof as you shall Judge convenient.[9]

Sir Thomas visited Winterton a few days later and found that the only thing to be done was to move the Small Light bodily further back up the beach. A working party was recruited locally and the lighthouse was set up in its new position before the month was out. A "Notice to Mariners" was published in the London Gazette on March 1st.

Unfortunately a vessel was lost on Winterton Ness almost immediately and the Trinity Brethren were openly blamed. In view of the serious implications, two Elder Brethren were sent to inspect the site and satisfy themselves that the Small Light was well clear of the Tower Light and standing on a firm foundation. They submitted their findings to Trinity House on 24th April:

> "They have set it soe wide of the Great Light that Shipps in that channel may sail safe, and they have secured it soe well that they think it may stand this 20 yeares."[10]

This estimate proved highly optimistic, for within three years the sea was again threatening to wash the lighthouse away. This time there was no Sir Thomas Allin to ask for good advice, as he had died in October, 1685. Instead the Corporation sent instructions to the agent at Yarmouth to have some local builders survey the Small Light and recommend how it might best be preserved. The result of this survey reached Trinity House on 7th January, 1686. There was no hope of saving the lighthouse in its present position. The sea was gaining so rapidly that the Small Light would have to be withdrawn by at least two hundred yards, but this could only be done if the Tower Light, now in the hands of a new owner, was moved correspondingly. Following the death of Alderman Gore the lease had passed to his son-in-law, Sir Edward Turnour, of Little Parndon in Essex. Now if the Trinity Brethren were to be able to continue their Small Light it was imperative that Sir Edward Turnour should co-operate. If he refused to move his Tower Light the Small Light could not be moved either.

This situation was debated at a meeting of the Trinity House Court in February 1686. It was decided to go about obtaining two plots of ground at Winterton and to leave it to local gossip to carry the news to Sir Edward Turnour that Trinity House was intending to set up a pair of leading lights of their own. It was purely bluff. The Brethren had no intention of setting up any more lights if it could be avoided, but were merely relying on Sir Edward Turnour taking these token preparations seriously. The last thing he would want was Trinity House to come out in open competition with him. He would be forced to oppose such a move to the limit of his resources, and Sir Edward Turnour's resources, as will be seen in the section on Orford Ness, were dwindling fast away. A few days later one of the Corporation's senior members, Captain Rutter, left for Winterton, charged with the task of acquiring the necessary parcels of land. This was accomplished without too much difficulty, especially as one of them happened to belong to the keeper of the Small Light, Mr Thomas White, who readily agreed to a price of ten pounds and was instrumental also in obtaining the second plot, which belonged to a widow of the parish.

The news did not take long to reach Sir Edward Turnour. Early in April he called personally at Trinity House "on the occasion of his hearing that the Corporation was about to do something prejudicial to his interests at Winterton." He was told that what the Corporation were intending was solely in the interests of navigation, and Sir Edward went away fully convinced that his worse fears were justified.

The whole business was allowed to remain at a complete standstill throughout that summer. The two plots were left standing idle, no move was made to erect any lighthouses on them, nor was any attempt made to protect the existing Small Light, and Sir Edward Turnour was left to stew.

Matters were again brought to a head by the onset of winter and the inevitable gales and storms. On 15th November Thomas White, whose business head was evidently not matched by his scholarly hand, wrote to Trinity House to report that the Small Light had sustained further damage. He received a reply from Samuel Hunter, Clerk of Trinity House, dated 20th November:

> "You are directed to get an able workman or two from Yarmouth to survey our lighthouse and give an opinion of how it may be secured; whether by driving piles about it or otherwise for this winter, which pray give me an account of forthwith. You are directed to get somebody to write your letters and accounts for you because we cannot read your hand."

On the same day Thomas White was writing a second and more urgent letter reporting that the situation had worsened. The sea had undermined the bank on which the lighthouse stood and inflicted further damage on the structure of the tower. It was resolved that matters could be delayed no longer. As soon as conditions permitted the lighthouse would have to be moved. It was decided to summon Sir Edward Turnour to the next session of the Court and openly inform him of the Corporation's real intentions. Sir Edward Turnour attended Trinity House on 30th November. The Brethren's ruse had worked like a charm. He proved only too willing to agree to any proposal they cared to make. He was, he explained, interested only in doing what was for the good of Navigation and had no wish to offend the Trinity Brethren, for whom he had the greatest respect, his father having been a member of their Corporation.[11] He was quite prepared to move his Tower Lighthouse, although he did not think it wise to do so until after the winter was over.

It was arranged that with the coming of Spring both lighthouses would be set up in their new positions. Sir Edward readily agreed. He would do whatsoever they directed; let him but know how and when he should do it. All things would be prepared for erecting the Great Light in May. Such co-operation was unprecedented; the Brethren's bluff was paying dividends beyond their wildest hopes. More accustomed to defending their own actions with regard to erecting lighthouses, they now found themselves in a position actually to call the tune, a tune to which Sir Edward Turnour seemed disposed to dance most energetically.

The Brethren decided to press home their advantage while the going was good. Sir Edward was summoned to Trinity House again in February 1687. The Corporation, he was told, considered it desirable that he should build a completely new lighthouse of brickwork and masonry, and that his existing tower should be made to serve until the new structure was ready. Sir Edward raised no objection even to these exacting and costly demands. He would, he

Shipping off Winterton Ness, with the Thwart Lights seen in the distance.

Norfolk County Library

assured them, immediately apply himself to the task of providing materials. Building finally commenced in April and continued throughout the following summer. Sir Edward Turnour's new lighthouse took the form of an octagonal tower rising in three stages to a height of 70 feet. It stood on the edge of what was at that time a low sandy cliff, which added another 20 feet to the elevation of the coal fire surmounting the tower.

Throughout this time the Trinity Brethren had allowed the Small Light to fall into disuse, thereby attracting strong criticism from masters of vessels in the coasting trade who complained that the derelict tower was liable to cause confusion, and demanded that it should be moved out of sight. The Corporation gave instructions for it to be dragged bodily to a less conspicuous position, there to await the completion of the new high lighthouse. By mid-August the new tower was nearing completion and the Small Light was set up in relation to it. At the end of the month Thomas White informed the Trinity Brethren that both lighthouses were ready for service, and the Corporation gave orders for the lights to be kindled on the night of September 12th, 1687.

With the Winterton lights rebuilt and realigned, the northern entrance to Yarmouth Roads was adequately lit once more. The two lights on the Ness continued to serve as an alternative approach to the channel, primarily for the benefit of the local fishermen, and for this reason they were generally known as the "Fishermen's Lights". Alternatively, they became widely referred to as the "Thwart Lights", due to the fact that any vessel following their line of direction would be led in "thwart the tide."

The arrangement whereby Trinity House collected its own dues in respect of the Small Light was continued as before, and Sir Edward Turnour retained the benefit of the Thwart Lights, together with that of his new Tower Light. What this amounted to in total there is no means of knowing, but some indication may be gained from a set of accounts that has survived from the year 1709. For the twelve-month period ended at Michaelmas that year, the lights of Winterton and Orford Ness together, with all disbursements met, yielded to Sir Edward Turnour a nett profit of £981 4s. 0d.[12] The first map to show the lights on their new locations was issued in 1695. It was the work of Robert Morden and was produced as an illustration for Camden's *Britannia*. It marked the bearing of the two lights on the Ness, as well as the two lights in Winterton village, the rear one of which is designated the "New Fire Light". These were the four lights that Daniel Defoe was somewhat surprised to find on his visit here some years later.

The scouring of this section of coast still continued and in 1714 the front Thwart Light was washed away and had to be replaced. Soon after this, the first attempts were made to position lightvessels offshore to mark the channels through the sands. In 1732 a certain Dr David Avery obtained a patent to station a floating light at the Nore Sand in the Thames approaches, and followed it soon after with another at the Well. In protest at what they regarded as a violation of their authority, the Trinity Brethren petitioned the King and succeeded in getting Avery's grant withdrawn. Having thus asserted themselves, the Brethren promptly applied for the patent in their own name and in 1736 they leased it out again to Avery. So beneficial did these lightvessels prove to be that Avery was encouraged to go further and in 1738 he submitted a proposal for a lightship to be stationed off the Cockle Sand. To assist him in this enterprise he engaged the services of one Robert Hamblin, formerly a Lynn barber, but now a self-styled sea captain. Entrusting him with the sum of fifty pounds, Avery sent him to Yarmouth to solicit support from local mariners. But, according to John Whormby,[13] Hamblin arrived in Yarmouth purporting to be himself the promoter of the project. Armed with a set of wild and ridiculous plans, he took himself off to Winterton and caused such a flutter in an alehouse there with his fanatical talk that the overseer of the lights took him for a madman (which, in Whormby's opinion, he was).

At this point Trinity House stepped in and sent five Elder Brethren to Winterton to look into the whole affair. Their verdict was that it would be quite impracticable to position a floating light at the Cockle Sand owing to lack of searoom. Should the vessel break adrift from her moorings (as the "Well" had done, twice in three winters) there was nothing to prevent her from running ashore or being cast away on the sands. Instead it was decided to alter the alignment of the Thwart Lights, thereby achieving the same result.[14]

John Whormby's account also reveals that by this time the lights had been converted from candles to oil, with the exception of the Tower Light. This remained a coal fire and was still not glazed in. A further forty-five years were to pass before any improvement was introduced at the Tower Lighthouse, and even then it took a major disaster to bring it about. It happened on the night of 31st October, 1789, when a particularly severe storm struck the east coast, wreaking havoc along the shores of East Anglia and taking an appalling toll of ships and lives.

At the subsequent inquiry it was revealed that there had been some confusion between the Winterton lights and the Trinity House lights at nearby Caister. Instead of bringing together the front and rear light of each pair respectively, some shipmasters had lined up the front light of one with the rear light of the other, thereby following an utterly false course on to the sands. It became clear that profound measures were needed to ensure that such a thing never happened again. In particular, shipping interests in the north of England were anxious that a means should exist of marking the dangerous sands lying off Happisburgh (pronounced, and in nautical terms spelled, Haisbro'). A petition was now put forward by one Henry Taylor of North Shields, supported by merchants and masters from Newcastle, Whitby and

Scarborough, calling for a lighthouse to be set up on the cliffs close to Happisburgh village.

It was not the first time that this location had been considered for coast lights. John Whormby relates that a group of collier masters petitioned for a lighthouse here in 1720, but the wording of the proposal was so ambiguous that Trinity House returned it for clarification and the matter was never pursued. Now, seventy years later, the Trinity Brethren themselves applied for a patent to erect a pair of leading lights on this same site as a replacement for their Small Light at Winterton which they now proposed to discontinue. The patent was granted to them on 30th October 1790.

Winterton lighthouse about 1910. The field of currant bushes in the foreground is now a chalet park.
Norfolk County Library

Two circular towers were built, the high light being raised to a height of 94 feet and the low light some 20 feet shorter. Each was surmounted by a lantern containing oil lamps and reflectors, and when brought into line with each other they led vessels safely clear of the southern tip of the Haisbro' Sands. These lights were displayed for the first time on New Year's Day, 1791.[15]

With the closure of their Small Light, the Trinity Brethren ceased to hold any stake in the lighting at Winterton. Nevertheless, they still wielded advisory and supervisory powers over privately administered concessions, by which they could insist on acceptable standards of efficiency being maintained, and invoking these powers, the brethren now directed that Winterton Tower Light should be converted from a coal fire to an oil light. They made similar demands of the lessee of Cromer lighthouse at this time. Such an improvement at Winterton was long overdue. All the other lights there had been using oil as an illuminant for almost fifty years; John Whormby's account proves that. Yet the Tower Light, the principal light in the vicinity and the one required to be seen over the greatest distance, remained exactly as Sir Edward Turnour had built it in 1687 and essentially the same as when the station had first come into existence 175 years previously.

The Trinity Brethren made their recommendations known to the current owner of the lease, the recently created Lord Braybrooke. His lordship readily complied with these requirements, and the coal hearth, which had stood for so long at the summit of the Tower Lighthouse, now gave place to a glazed lantern housing a cluster of eleven reflectors, each with an oil burner set in its focal centre. The new light shone for the first time on the night of 23rd November, 1791. Unlike the new apparatus at Cromer, which revolved to produce an intermittent flash, Winterton shone a fixed, steady light, visible for 14 miles. Throughout the further 130 years that the station continued in service, and the subsequent improvements that were introduced, this fixed character remained a feature of Winterton lighthouse.

Lord Braybrooke died in 1797 and was succeeded by Richard Aldworth Neville, 2nd Lord Braybrooke. To the new holder of the title came also the lease of Winterton and Orford lights, with 29 years of the current term still outstanding.

The tide of opinion now began to run counter to the idea of privately-owned lighthouses and the further this lease ran its course, the more likely it began to appear that the grant would be placed in the hands of Trinity House as soon as it became free. The report by a Select Committee in 1822 advocating the surrender of all private grants, on expiration of their terms in being, made this seem even more of a certainty. It came as no surprise when Lord Braybrooke's advance application for a renewal was refused. His lordship appealed, on the grounds that he had not had sufficient time to recover the expenses he had incurred, not only at Winterton, but at Orford Ness also, where he had been obliged to build a new high light in 1792. The outlay must have been heavy indeed, if the cost had still not been recouped after more than thirty years, since at the time of this appeal the lights of Winterton and Orford Ness together were reputed to be earning an average of £13,414 per annum.[16] The eventual outcome was a further lease for a period of twenty-one years, commencing on 1st June, 1828. This renewal, however, stipulated certain changes from previous grants. It did not include the Thwart Lights, which had now been allowed to lapse. Furthermore, the rate of tolls was reduced by one halfpenny per ton, both here and at Orford, while from now on the Crown laid claim to half the nett profits.

The precise date at which the Thwart Lights were discontinued is not altogether certain. They were depicted as working lighthouses on a map made in 1803,[17] and they appeared also on a survey made in 1817 in preparation for the first edition of the one-inch Ordnance Survey series. For various reasons the issue of this map was delayed for almost twenty years, making it necessary for the original work to be updated prior to publication in 1837. Among the amendments made at this time was the deletion of Winterton Ness Lights. As near as can be said, then, the two Thwart Lights were discontinued at some time between 1817 (the date of the preliminary field survey) and 1828 (the date of Lord Braybrooke's extended lease). White's *Directory of Norfolk*, first published in 1834, records that the two derelict towers on the Ness were demolished about 1830.

It now seemed that the Trinity Brethren would have to wait until at least 1849 before another chance would occur to acquire this grant. In the event the opportunity came much earlier than expected. In 1836 came the Act of Parliament which brought an end to the era of private lighthouse ownership and gave to Trinity House powers to acquire by purchase the remaining leases which had eluded them for so long. The additional term granted in 1828 proved a costly one from the Trinity Brethren's point of view, since the length of the lease outstanding was an important factor in assessing the amount of compensation to be paid. The final figure placed on the unexpired portion of the lease, which had exactly twelve years and five months to run, together with the value of the lighthouse at Winterton and the two towers on Orford Ness, totalled £145,937. Of this, the sum of £37,896 was due to Lord Braybrooke and the remaining £108,040 represented the value of the Crown's interests.

With so many other stations coming into their possession at the same time, all of which required improvement if not complete renewal, Trinity House found itself under considerable financial strain, and Winterton had to

Left: Nearly a century after the Happisburgh low lighthouse was demolished its foundations were laid bare by cliff erosion.

Opposite: Happisburgh lighthouse about 1905, when it was lit by coal gas manufactured on the premises. The retort house and two small gasholders can be seen.

take its turn with the rest. At last, in 1840, a new tower took the place of Sir Edward Turnour's old hexagonal lighthouse, which was then demolished. The new building was of brick and masonry, circular in shape and raised to a height of 62 feet. It was unique, perhaps, in that it was built without taper, the walls retaining the same diameter and thickness from base to gallery. The low ridge on which it stood raised the light to an elevation of 97 feet above sea level and the cluster of eleven oil burners and reflectors projected its rays over a distance of 17 miles to seaward. It was lit for the first time in the early autumn of 1840, and the final phase in the story of Winterton Lights had begun.

In 1843 the lighting of Yarmouth Roads was further augmented by the placing of a floating light at the Cockle Sand, just as David Avery had advocated many years before. In 1863 the oil lamps and reflectors at Winterton were replaced by a triple-wick Argand apparatus with a prismatic lens. Soon after 1880 the front light of the pair at Happisburgh was found to be in immediate danger due to the erosion of the coast. Accordingly it was discontinued in May, 1883, and the following month the tower was demolished. The high light was retained as a single working lighthouse, and still remains in service as the Happisburgh lighthouse of the present day.

While encroachments by the sea were having such profound effects at Happisburgh, only a few miles down the coast at Winterton the trend was reversed. This low-lying strip of coast lent itself readily to the planting of marram grass, the properties of which tough and prolific marine grass had long been realised by the Dutch, whose own coasts were so similar in nature. On the strength of their experience, attempts were made in the late eighteenth century to establish this form of vegetation along the sandy, unstable beaches

of East Anglia. Local estate maps made in the eighteenth and early nineteenth centuries show this sector of coast to be extensively planted with young marram. As an experiment in coast protection it was an unqualified success. The tufts of grass easily took root and flourished, binding the beaches with a fibrous matting below the surface and immobilising the hills of driven sand above. At Winterton, a barrier of dunes rose up between high-water mark and the low ridge on which the lighthouse stood, leaving a sweeping valley in between. This ridge spread rapidly south towards the neighbouring village of Hemsby. By the turn of the present century this valley had become The Valley, and although it is nowadays claimed by Hemsby for the delight of its summer visitors, it is a feature whose origins rightfully belong to Winterton.

By the First World War, more than four hundred yards of valley and dunes separated Winterton lighthouse from the sea and the floating lights out to sea had become so numerous and efficient, and the channel into Yarmouth Roads so well buoyed, that the presence of a lighthouse at Winterton was no longer necessary. In 1921 it was decided to close the station down, along with its counterpart at Hunstanton which had similarly out-lived its usefulness.

At daybreak one morning in the autumn of 1921, Winterton Tower Light

Opposite: A distant view of Winterton lighthouse at the beginning of the century showing the extensive area of dunes between the lighthouse and the sea which gradually built up over the years.

Right: Although it has long ceased to exhibit a light, Winterton lighthouse still serves as an aid to navigation; note the Racon beacon on the summit of the tower.

was extinguished for the last time, so bringing an end to more than three centuries of sea lights displayed from this remote and notorious point of the coast. On no fewer than four occasions during that time, the Trinity Brethren had established lights here, and as many times again had relinquished them, twice under duress and twice of their own accord.

On 25th January, 1922, the former lighthouse, shorn of its lantern and gutted of its equipment, was sold by auction at the Star Hotel, Great Yarmouth. Between then and the outbreak of the Second World War the premises were used as a seaside residence, but in 1939 the site was commandeered by the military authorities, who added a brickwork look-out above the level of the gallery. Apart from this, the end of the war found the tower substantially unchanged and still bearing traces of the overall red coat which had once distinguished it from its striped neighbour at Happisburgh. It then reverted to a private residence, in which capacity it served for the next twenty years.

Finally, in 1965, the former lighthouse again came on the market and was purchased by the proprietors of the adjoining holiday hotel, of which it now forms a part.

CHAPTER THREE

Orford Ness

He said there was a lighthouse there,
Where lonely by the sea,
Men lived to guard that moving light,
And trim the lamps for me.
(*The Lighthouse* — Marjorie Wilson)

THE River Alde first sees the light of day in the heart of the Suffolk countryside not far from the village of Badingham. From here its leisurely and meandering course eventually carries it to the coast at Aldeburgh where, having come to within a few yards of the sea, the river veers suddenly southwards and runs for a further eleven miles parallel with the shore before finally turning to enter the sea at Shingle Street. Needless to say this is a route which the river does not pursue voluntarily, but one which has been forced on it by radical changes in the configuration of the coastline.

It is a feature of all headlands and outcrops along the east coast of England that they develop in a north to south direction. Two examples stand out beyond all others. One is at the point where the River Humber enters the sea. Here a slender ridge of shingle and dune has built up, reaching southwards from the coast of Holderness to form a curved fang in the Humber's mouth. The other is Orford Ness, with its roots at Aldeburgh, its tip at Shingle Street, and the characteristic hooked outline on its seaward side. When this barrier first began to develop the free outfall of the Alde was impeded, resulting in a widening of the river a short distance upstream. This process, technically known as "ponding back", is much in evidence on several East Anglian rivers. The restricted mouth of the Yare, for instance, has resulted in the tidal expanse of Breydon Water to the rear of Great Yarmouth, while the River Blyth has similarly ponded back upriver from Southwold.

The distribution of Roman remains found in the vicinity of Aldeburgh suggests that the Alde had already ponded back by the time of the Roman occupation, indicating that some form of bottleneck existed at the river's mouth. As the years went by that mouth became completely closed off by the advancing shingle ridge, which forced the river to turn and follow it down the coast. Until the spit advanced Orford, five miles to the south, had been an

Orford Ness lighthouse built by the 1st Lord Braybrooke in 1792, seen after it had become the first of Britain's lighthouses to be fully automated.

53

obscure and unimportant settlement. It fronted the sea from which it drew its living, while its inshore waters provided a roadstead in which ships of burden could shelter in times of storm. Gradually the great shingle spit bearing down from the north transformed Orford into a sheltered haven and a flourishing township. In 1165 King Henry II ordered the building of a great castle here to stand guard over the haven entrance and uphold royal authority in this part of eastern England. The extreme tip of the Ness had by this time reached a point in roughly the same latitude as the site chosen for the castle. Unfortunately the spit did not halt here, and its further development resulted in Orford being sealed off from direct communication with the sea.

There came a time when the spit veered suddenly south-westwards, following the natural trend of the coast, creating a pronounced knuckle-bend to its seaward side. Evidence of this first appears on a map by an unknown cartographer in the reign of Henry VIII. Although the bend is highly over-emphasised and incorrectly placed to the north of Orford Castle, it does at least show that it was well in evidence when the map was made. It was left to an estate surveyor, John Norden, in 1601 to place the point of recurvature in its true position, slightly south of a line drawn due east to west through Orford church and castle. That is where it is still located today. It is the only point along this eleven miles of shingle barrier that is properly called a Ness. For navigational purposes it is considered to be the northern extremity of the Thames Estuary. It also forms the focal centre of this account, for it is here, on this isolated and inaccessible cape, that the story of Orford lights is set.

*   *   *   *   *   *

The sheltered inshore passage through Yarmouth and Lowestoft Roads is continued down the Suffolk coast by a further series of channels sheltered by a chain of sandbanks reaching down to Harwich. To the collier fleets and other craft navigating the coasts of East Anglia in the days of sail, these sands came as a mixed blessing. They served well to break the full force of the sea and to create a sheltered roadstead close inshore, but in times of gale and storm the sands became a hidden menace, ready to swallow any vessel luckless enough to be driven within their grasp.

In the early part of the seventeenth century a substantial build-up of the banks off Orford Ness evidently took place. By 1618 the casualty rate had become so high that the collier trade appealed to Trinity House for lights to be provided. Nothing came of this appeal, and it was another nine years before the matter came to a head once more as a result of the events of 28th October, 1627. The great storm on this, Saint Simon's and Saint Jude's Day, was among the worst ever to strike the Suffolk coast. It reached the full height of its fury during the dark hours just before dawn, when a fleet of laden colliers was groping its way uncertainly through the shoal waters off Aldeburgh. Many vessels were swept on to Aldeburgh Napes, while others were carried southwards on to the Shipwash Sand. Thirty-two wrecks were cast up on Orford Ness with scarcely a survivor among their crews. As a result of this disaster the bailiffs of Aldeburgh raised a further petition, supported by the signatures of as many merchants and masters as they could muster, calling for lights to be set up on Orford Ness. This petition followed the usual protracted course of presentation to the Privy Council and submission to the Brethren of Trinity House for comment.

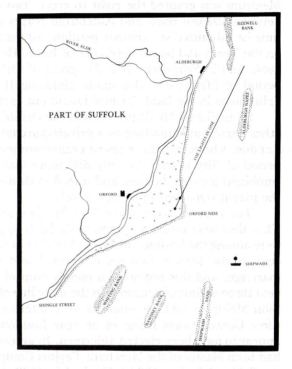

These formalities succeeded in delaying matters for upwards of three years. It was during this time, while the various interested parties were preoccupied with wrangling, that the owner of the Winterton lights, Sir John Meldrum, decided to take a hand. Supported by local shipmasters and fishermen who were tiring of the long delay, Meldrum submitted a petition to King Charles I craving the grant for himself. He would, he declared, be content with one penny per ton on all passing ships as he already was at Winterton, and furthermore he would undertake to maintain the lights "without charge upon traders for coals and fishermen".[1] As an additional concession Meldrum offered to make a grant for the benefit of the town of Aldeburgh[2] from the revenue he received.

As an original follower of James I into England, John Meldrum, "this thrice-honourable Scottish patriot", as a contemporary writer described him,[3] could always count on a sympathetic hearing at Court. In 1621 his bid to retain ownership of the Winterton grant had been upheld in the face of the strongest opposition from the Trinity Brethren. In the following year he received a knighthood at the hands of James and had since rendered distinguished service in several campaigns. The outcome of his petition for the lights of Orford Ness was practically a foregone conclusion. In February, 1634, Meldrum was granted the right to erect "two temporary lighthouses to lead between Sizewell Bank and Aldeburgh Napes in the north", and about that time he submitted yet another petition, asking permission to erect lighthouses on the North and South Forelands of Kent. He finally received this patent in 1636, and in February, 1637, his grant of Orford Ness was confirmed for a period of fifty years. This made Meldrum the largest individual owner of lighthouses in the land, Trinity House not excepted.

Immediately Meldrum received the Orford grant he disposed of it and his other interest at Winterton to a private purchaser, Alderman Gerard Gore, of London, who received a renewed grant commencing on 13th April, 1637, for a period of fifty years. The only difference was that the two leases were now combined into one holding and stayed so throughout the rest of the time that the patent remained in private hands.

The known history of the Gore family is somewhat sketchy and confused. That they were opulent merchants is fairly apparent, as is the fact that they were among the leading citizens of London in their day. In the early sixteenth century the ancient families of Jerrard and Gore became united through marriage, and this produced a goodly crop of Gerard Gores throughout the next three or four generations in the male line of descent. At the time when Sir John Meldrum sold his interests at Winterton and Orford Ness there were three Gerard Gores living in or near London, although only two of them appear to have been elected aldermen. In an earlier generation a Gerard Gore had been Master of the Merchant Taylors Company in 1567 and alderman for the Bridge Ward in 1574.[4] He died in 1607, leaving eight sons. Predictably one was christened Gerard. He is described as "gentleman of St Clement Danes in Middlesex" and became a warden of the Merchant Taylors Company, where he is referred to as Alderman Gerard Gore the elder. He could not have been the purchaser of the lights, however, for he died in 1660 and there is evidence to show that in 1663, as a result of complaints over the ill-keeping of Orford lights, Alderman Gore was commanded to appear before a Court at Trinity House.

Another of the eight sons was William Gore, who lived at Tottenham and who became Sheriff of London in 1615. By his marriage to Elizabeth Fowler of Islington he had a son, Gerard, who was admitted to the Middle Temple in 1626. This Gerard Gore died in 1671, bequeathing his estate to his wife.

Nowhere in his will is there any mention of lighthouses, nor is there any record of Gerard Gore of Tottenham ever being created an alderman.[5] This leaves a third Gerard Gore, described as "merchant of the City of London" and mentioned in the lists of Merchant Taylors as Alderman Gerard Gore the younger. His father was Sir John Gore, Lord Mayor of London in 1624-25. Gerard was the eldest son and inherited the family merchant and shipping interests. He was elected alderman for the Ward of Farringdon Without, largest of the newly-created wards lying outside the city walls. He was the owner of two large estates in the country, Shillinglee Park, on the Surrey-Sussex border, and Down Place near Godalming. This, we may be almost certain, was the man who now became possessed of the lights of Winterton and Orford Ness, and from this point John Meldrum ceases to feature in this account.

It may be of interest to record that Meldrum went on to play a prominent part in the Civil Wars, in which, it will be remembered, he inexplicably took sides with Parliament. Having distinguished himself at Portsmouth, Manchester and Hull, he was eventually assigned to the seige of Scarborough and was mortally wounded while storming its castle in May, 1645.

The two lights which Alderman Gore now built out on the most seaward point of the Ness were of timber and stood in line with each other to indicate a safe passage through the narrow gap between Sizewell Bank and Aldeburgh Napes. The rear light of the pair was the customary coal fire which served the dual purpose of marking the precise location of the Ness and at the same time acting as a high light to the candle lantern of the lower lighthouse.

In the early stages of his lease Gerard Gore appointed a woman to be lightkeeper, and soon had cause to regret it. Her father, it seems, was one of the original keepers and on his death the woman's husband, John Bradshaw, was allowed to replace him. Bradshaw, too, soon died, whereupon Alderman Gore, out of sympathy for his widow no doubt, agreed to her taking her husband's place. The performance of her duties by the widow Bradshaw may best be judged by the following letter signed by Alderman Gore in 1648:

According to my promise you have enjoyed the Light now till Xmas and I have had more complaints in this half-year than ever I had in your father or husband's time. I did not think you would have been so careless but I excuse it because you are a woman. My will is that you deliver the House and Light and all things as such belong to the House and Light to the attention of the Bailiffs of the Town of Aldeburgh, so not doubting of your performance therein, I rest

Yours
Gerard Gore.

Alderman Gore and his wife Sarah had an only daughter who took her mother's name and who was, of course, sole heiress to the family estates. Under the law as it then stood, a woman on her marriage forfeited all her possessions and entitlements to her husband, so that when the young and comely Sarah Gore married Edward Turnour, of Parndon in Essex, she brought him the prospect of a substantial inheritance. The Turnours were a family whose roots were deep in the county of Suffolk, where they had lived for generations at Haverhill. They were of French origin, but had for long been settled in these parts and had acquired considerable wealth from their interests in the wool trade. During the sixteenth century their influence spread into Essex, when an Edward Turnour of an earlier generation married Martha Hanchet, of the village of Great Parndon. From this line descended Arthur Turnour, who entered the legal profession and rose to the status of a serjeant-at-law. He married Anne Jermy, of Gunton in Norfolk.

To Arthur Turnour and Anne in 1616 was born Edward Turnour. This was the Edward Turnour who married Sarah, only daughter of Alderman Gerard Gore. Up to now, the Turnours, although otherwise prosperous and well respected, were not a family of widespread repute. The transition from

"Where lonely by the sea . . ." Orford Ness lighthouse isolated on the far tip of the Ness, while in the middle distance the river severs the headland from Orford village.   *D. J. Leech*

modest merchants to landed gentry had been a long, slow process, covering the span of several generations. Even now no member of the family had been rewarded with the grant of a title or similar honour, nor had any of them found favour at Court. Edward Turnour was soon to change all that.

He married Sarah Gore about the year 1644 and by her had six children, only four of whom survived infancy. By the outbreak of the Civil War, Edward Turnour was an established lawyer with premises in Threadneedle Street and all appeared set fair for the future. He had every prospect of succeeding one day to the property at Little Parndon, while his wife's inheritance would bring to him the inestimable wealth of the Gore family, together with their large estates in Sussex. But fate, having smiled for so long on the fortunes of the house of Turnour, now dealt a bitter blow. On 19th February, 1651, at the untimely age of 27, Sarah Turnour died, leaving her husband and their four surviving children. Some authorities state that Sir Edward Turnour only had one daughter and two sons, but this does not agree with an inscription in Little Parndon church which reads: "Here lieth the body of Mrs Sarah Turnour wife of Edward Turnour by whom he had six children whereof four survived her . . . She was the daughter and heir apparent of Gerard Gore of the city of London esq."

Meanwhile, Edward Turnour's career went from strength to strength. In 1654 he entered the world of politics and was returned as member for Essex in the election of 1658. At the Restoration in 1660 he received a knighthood at the hands of King Charles II. In the election of 1661 he was elected to serve for Hertford and was chosen as Speaker of the House of Commons.

Alderman Gore's lease of the lights had now run half its course, and this was seized upon by Sir Edward Turnour as an appropriate opportunity to petition for a renewal of the grant when the current term ended in 1687. This was done with the full knowledge and approval of his father-in-law, who was now more than 70 years of age and unlikely, therefore, to see the termination of his lease. As a result of this petition, on 15th October, 1661, a grant was made to Sir Edward Turnour to continue the lights at Winterton and Orford Ness on expiration of the term in being. This grant, "a personal reward for services to the Crown", was to be for a period of 33 years if the current lease ran its full course. But if, for any reason, the lease fell prematurely vacant, then Sir Edward's renewal was to be for a term of 60 years, commencing from the date of such voidance.[6] Having secured this grant, Sir Edward set about consolidating his position by purchasing outright the land on which the existing lighthouses stood, together with the ground affording access to them. At Orford Ness he acquired a sizeable portion of the King's Marshes, while at Winterton he purchased virtually the whole of the local manorial estate.

In May, 1670, Sir Edward became Solicitor General and during the following year was appointed Lord Chief Baron of the Exchequer. In this capacity his portrait was commissioned by the Corporation of London and hung in the Guildhall. In the event Sir Edward did not live to enjoy the benefit of his grant. He died on circuit at Bedford in March, 1676, and was buried with other members of his family in Little Parndon church. The estate now devolved to his eldest son, also named Edward.

The younger Edward Turnour was born in 1643. He became an even greater favourite with Charles II than his father had been, and received a knighthood at the early age of twenty-one. In 1667 he married Lady Isabella Keith, daughter of the Earl Marshal of Scotland, and the eldest child of this marriage was a son, to whom Charles II became godfather. Needless to say, the infant was christened Charles. Unfortunately the younger Sir Edward Turnour had none of the wisdom or force of character of his father and shortly after coming into his inheritance fell deeply into debt. It was not long before the various properties and estates acquired by Sir Edward Turnour, the elder, were all heavily mortgaged.

Into these thriftless and insolvent hands passed, in due course, the Winterton and Orford lease. Precisely when this happened is not apparent, since the date of Alderman Gore's death cannot be determined. What the evidence does show is that the outstanding portion of Alderman Gore's term passed into the possession of Sir Edward Turnour, junior, some time prior to 1685, for in that year he had already mortgaged it for the sum of £5,890.[7] When in 1686 the Trinity Brethren were forced to move their Small Light at Winterton and required the Tower Light to be shifted correspondingly it was Sir Edward Turnour, not Gerard Gore, whom they dealt with, although Gore's lease still had fifteen months to run at this point. On 13th April, 1687, on the termination of the original lease, Sir Edward Turnour entered into possession of the extended lease left to him by his father.

There now began the most disastrous period of lightkeeping in the history of this or any other station on the coasts of England. Orford lights, due to their remote and inaccessible situation, had never been the easiest of stations to supervise and back in Gerard Gore's time they had been the subject of frequent complaint. The minuted proceedings of the Trinity House Court, and the Turnour family's correspondence preserved in the West Sussex Record Office at Chichester, show that under Sir Edward Turnour's ownership such complaints became almost constant. In October, 1688, the two agents, Thomas Willes and Thomas Wall, sought to defend themselves against allegations that the lights were ill-kept and frequently unlit by informing Sir Edward that "the east winds make the sea darken the light"—whatever that was supposed to mean.[8] It was inevitable that such an unsatisfactory state of affairs would, sooner or later, render Sir Edward liable to be usurped by a rival contender for the patent and in April, 1695, when the outstanding term had been reduced to exactly twenty-five years, a petition came before the Privy

Council from one Ralph Grey, craving a renewal of the lease on its termination in 1720.

Ralph Grey was one of three children of the marriage between the 2nd Lord Grey of Werke, Northumberland, and Catherine Forde, of Hartling in Sussex. In addition to Ralph, who was named after his father, there was an elder son who took his mother's maiden name of Forde and a sister who shared her mother's christian name of Catherine. History has little to say to the credit of Lord Forde Grey. In an age of controversy and political instability he stands out as possibly the most controversial, and, some may say, the most unstable, figure of all. He was brought to trial on numerous occasions, to face such a variety of charges as inciting a riot, eloping with his wife's sister, and assaulting the lord mayor of London, not to mention the more serious counts of conspiracy and high treason. Having turned evidence against his associates in the Duke of Monmouth's rebellion, Forde Grey set out to work his way into a position of high favour with William III.

Compared with Forde Grey's nefarious and turncoat activities, the career of his younger brother, Ralph, seems tame and uneventful. But Ralph Grey, by less turbulent means, had already secured for himself a position of trust and favour equal to anything that his brother enjoyed. Ever since the new king had landed in the west country as William of Orange, Ralph Grey had been his close follower and loyal supporter. In the defeat of James II at the Battle of the Boyne, and in every campaign of the continuing war against France, he had rendered distinguished service. In 1692 that service brought its first reward when he was appointed Auditor of Crown Revenues for Wales. It could at least be said that Ralph Grey had earned rather than curried the King's favour, and that favour was now to stand him in good stead in his bid to obtain the Winterton and Orford grant.

The petition was referred by the Privy Council to the Surveyor of Crown Lands, Mr Samuel Travers, calling on him to furnish details of the existing lease and an assessment of the rate to be charged for a new one. Samuel Travers submitted his report early in April, 1695:

"I have no account of the profits of these lighthouses in my office, nor do I find any proceedings there towards the passing the last grant, but I have enquired into the value thereof and am credibly informed that the same yields *communibus annis* 1,200 pounds a year above all charges and deductions, at which rate I value the desired reversion at 3,000 pounds."

On the strength of this report, Ralph Grey was granted his extension, not at the £3,000 suggested by Samuel Travers, but for "750 pounds only and in consideration of the said Grey's good services".[9] The Royal Warrant was issued on 17th April, 1695. Events had moved so quickly that the Trinity Brethren do not appear to have had sufficient time to voice their objections.

Someone who did object, naturally, was Sir Edward Turnour. He and Ralph Grey were summoned to a hearing at the Treasury Chambers in Whitehall on 3rd May.[10] Sir Edward's case laid great emphasis on his ownership of the lands and rights of way, he doubtless reasoning that there was some truth in the old saying that possession was nine-tenths of the law. When Ralph Grey came to state his case he completely rejected this contention. He pointed out that when Sir Edward's father had first acquired the grant in 1661 he had no right to the lands either, but came to an agreement with the owners, which was precisely what he (Ralph Grey) was asking now.

The Lords of the Treasury directed that Grey and Sir Edward should refer their case to the Solicitor General and submit to his arbitration. This was a verdict that went badly for Sir Edward Turnour, who was more concerned at that particular moment with trying to keep a roof over his head. Any solution involving ready cash was out of the question for him, and seizing on this weak spot Ralph Grey came up with an offer which the Solicitor-General accepted as a just and reasonable proposition. Ralph Grey's offer was that he would allow Sir Edward the opportunity to purchase the grant from him at a realistic market price. On 7th June, 1695, exactly one month after the matter was referred to the Solicitor-General, Ralph Grey issued a solemn declaration upon his honour that this offer would stand for a period of six months to be reckoned from that day.[11] Outwardly it appeared a most noble and considerate gesture, in reality it amounted to an ultimatum. If Sir Edward failed to take this offer up he would be finished. To do so would mean raising sufficient cash to purchase the grant outright, in addition to the money already required to redeem his mortgages, and all within the space of six months. He had no chance of doing so, as everyone knew full well.

Ralph Grey certainly knew it. So confident was he that he departed for the continent to attend the King in his latest campaign against the French, leaving the matter in the hands of two executives, George Davenant and Richard Neville. George Davenant was a friend and legal advisor, while Richard Neville was Grey's brother-in-law, being the husband of his younger sister Catherine. The six-month grace allowed to Sir Edward Turnour expired on 7th December, 1695. Christmas came and went with no sign of Sir Edward making any attempt to redeem his mortgaged estates or to sell them, and consequently, on 30th January, 1696, the Letters Patent of William III were issued in the names of Richard Neville and George Davenant for the renewed term to commence on 13th April, 1720, leaving Sir Edward Turnour still threatening that when the time came he would sue for trespass anyone who dared to approach his lighthouses. That time was still more than twenty-four years distant, however, and much could happen before then.

Ralph Grey returned to England early in 1697 to receive further recognition of his services. In April of that year he was appointed governor of

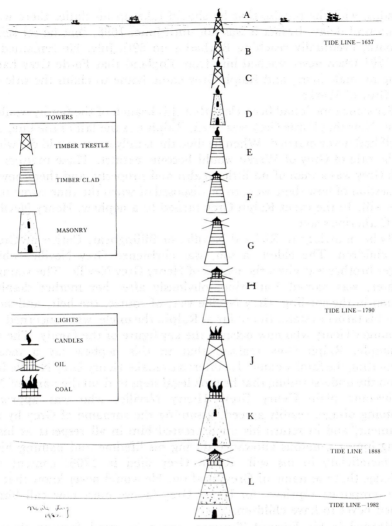

TIDE LINE – 1637

TIDE LINE – 1790

TIDE LINE 1888

TIDE LINE – 1982

TOWERS

TIMBER TRESTLE

TIMBER CLAD

MASONRY

LIGHTS

CANDLES

OIL

COAL

A. Alderman Gore (1637). Front light in relation to J. Moved back 1690. Washed away 1691.

B. Sir Edward Turnour (1691). Replacement for A. Washed away 1709.

C. Sir Edward Turnour (1709). Replacement for B. Demolished 1720.

D. Henry Grey (1720). Front light in relation to K. Washed away 1724.

E. Henry Grey (1724). Replacement for D. Washed away 1730.

F. Henry Grey (1730). Replacement for E. Burned down 1731.

G. Henry Grey (1731). Replacement for F. Burned down 1732.

H. Henry Grey (1732). Replacement for G. Threatened by the sea and demolished 1792.

J. Alderman Gore (1637). High light in relation to A. B. and C. Demolished 1720.

K. Henry Grey (1720). High light in relation to D. E. F. G. and H. Became front light in relation to L. 1792. Abandoned to the sea 1889.

L. Sir John Griffin-Griffin, 1st Lord Braybrooke (1792). High light in relation to K. Became single light in 1889. Still in service 1982.

Barbados, with the proviso that he should take up his duties there with the minimum of delay. In fact it was not until June, 1698, that he set sail from Plymouth, eventually reaching Barbados on 29th July. He remained there until 1701 when news reached him from England that Forde Grey had died leaving no male heirs, and Ralph Grey came home to claim the title of 4th Lord Grey of Werke.

For some time it had been clear that this branch of the family would soon die out. Now that Forde Grey was dead, Ralph was the last of the line, and he himself had never married. When he died the family name would die with him and the title of Grey of Werke would become extinct. These matters apart, Ralph Grey was a man of no little wealth and property, and there now arose the question of how these were to be disposed of when the time came to draw up his will. In the event Ralph Grey turned to a nephew, Henry Neville, his sister Catherine's son.

By her marriage to Richard Neville, of Billingbear, Catherine Grey had three children. The eldest, a son, was christened Grey Neville, while his younger brother was given the names of Henry Grey Neville. The youngest, a daughter, was named Katherine, obviously after her mother despite the variation in the spelling. Grey Neville was, of course, the heir, and stood to inherit his father's estate. But so far as Ralph, the uncle, was concerned, it was the younger Henry who now became the key figure of the family. The reason was simple. Ralph Grey realised that in this nephew lay a means of perpetuating the family name. He offered to make Henry Grey Neville his sole heir, on the understanding that he took legal steps to drop the name of Neville and become plain Henry Grey. Henry Neville, who was approaching his-coming-of-age, readily agreed, assuming the surname of Grey by Act of Parliament, and in return his uncle treated him in all respects as his heir, making him a generous allowance during his lifetime and naming him the chief beneficiary in his will. Ralph Grey died in 1706, content in the knowledge that the name of Grey lived on. He would never know that it was only a temporary reprieve, for Henry Grey (as we must now call him) was destined never to have children.

Meanwhile Sir Edward Turnour, more by good fortune than good management, contrived to hold on to his grant. Now that there was no longer any prospect of his retaining the lease beyond the current term, the standard of supervision fell even lower, particularly at Orford, where the lights became more complained of than any others in the kingdom. In January, 1690, the junior keeper, who had only recently been employed at the lighthouse, was carried off by the press gang. Owing to the encroachments of the sea the front tower had become threatened during the winter of 1690 and was moved back a distance of 30 yards, halving the distance that had separated the lights when first built. The sea continued to advance, carrying the tower completely away early in 1691, and Sir Edward Turnour then replaced it with another of almost identical design.

In 1700 when the coasting trade registered its disapproval of the Orford lights by refusing to contribute any further tolls towards them Trinity House ordered its Clerk, Samuel Hunter, to proceed to Orford and investigate. Hunter was one of the most highly esteemed Clerks ever to serve the Corporation. "Our trusty and well beloved Samuel Hunter," as James II once described him, had the honour of being personally nominated into office by that Sovereign in 1685. In his report on the situation at Orford Mr Hunter had some harsh things to say concerning the state of the lights. He found the "Great Light" in a sorry state of repair, with a fire basket too small to contain an adequate fire. The low light, burning a single candle, was in Mr Hunter's opinion quite insufficient. He was severely critical also of the short distance separating the two towers.

The Trinity Brethren forwarded this report to Sir Edward Turnour with a demand that the situation be rectified. Any improvement that did result was only minimal, however, doing little to stem the constant flow of complaints. A larger fire basket was installed in deference to Samuel Hunter's recommendations, but caused immediate problems by setting fire to the interior of the lantern. The overseer, John Hooke, eventually persuaded Sir Edward Turnour to revert to a smaller grate. In a letter to Sir Edward in December, 1701, Hooke confirmed that this had achieved the desired effect, and that the light was "100 times better now than with that great troublesome, Expensive and Dangerous Grate".

In 1702 a party of Elder Brethren led by Sir Henry Johnson, owner of the famous Blackwall shipyard where so many of the East Indiamen were laid down, visited the lighthouses. Their findings endorsed all that Samuel Hunter had said, and as a result Sir Edward Turnour was reported to the Privy Council.

On 23rd June, 1707, the crew of a French privateer landed on the Ness and attacked the lighthouses, causing much damage and making off with the keepers' bedding. Again during the following year Sir Edward Turnour received similar unwelcome news from the unscholarly pen of John Hooke:

"There have been a privateer Shoote at the Lithouse and have Broke all the glass". [12]

In 1709 the sea again carried away the front tower, forcing Sir Edward to provide a replacement which managed to survive for the remaining eleven years of the lease. These years followed slowly one upon the other, punctuated by protests and allegations of neglect, while the Brethren of Trinity House did their best to coax and prod Sir Edward Turnour into fulfilling his obligations at Orford.

Eventually the year 1720 arrived, bringing with it much speculation as to how Sir Edward would react to his lighthouse being taken over. Sir Edward reacted exactly as he had reacted many years before, repeating his threat to bring legal proceedings against anyone who set foot on his land.

Doubtless some people would have been thoroughly intimidated by Sir Edward's attitude and would either have meekly withdrawn or tried to bargain with him. The impetuous and headstrong Henry Grey was not one of them. Henry Grey Neville, alias Harry Neville, alias Henry Grey, has passed into history as the undisputed black sheep of that otherwise conventional family of landed gentry, the Nevilles of Billingbear. His was the sixth successive generation to hold the manorial estate near Waltham St Lawrence in Berkshire. This land, which once formed part of Windsor Forest, was first granted during the sixteenth century to Sir Henry Neville as a reward for his services as a privy councillor. It was he who established Billingbear as the family seat, building the fine mansion of warm red brick and laying out the park with its avenue of gigantic oaks, renowned throughout England. Henry Grey Neville, later to become Henry Grey, was born here on 17th August, 1683. A rebel by nature, like his uncle, Forde, before him, Henry Grey came to be regarded as a mild eccentric; the family buffoon whom nobody took too seriously. There was always something of the showman about him; he loved the limelight. Above all he was a hopeless spendthrift who allowed money to run through his hands like water.

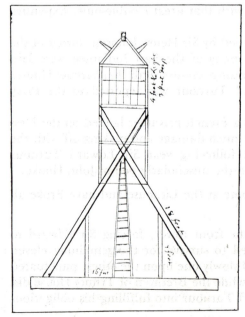

A plan of the front light proposed to replace that at Orford Ness washed away in 1709. It is the tower marked "C" in the illustration on page 63. *West Sussex Record Office*

He seems to have lived for the most part in London, where he had a wide circle of friends to whom he was always known as Harry Neville. In 1701, when Forde Grey's estates were divided up, he had come into possession of Morwick in Northumberland. It proved to be a liability rather than an asset, for with it went an enormous debt. Not that this worried Henry Grey unduly, for he chose to ignore the whole affair. To him the tithes and rents from Morwick were just one more source of income, to be spent to the last penny. This was the man who now laid claim to the Orford lights, a man with even less of a business head on his shoulders than Sir Edward Turnour.

To do him justice, it should be said that Henry Grey took his responsibilities as a lighthouse proprietor rather more seriously than he took most other things in life. In an initial burst of enthusiasm he seems to have made a determined effort to rectify the situation at Orford. Well in advance of his lease maturing, new lightkeepers and a local overseer had been recruited. But when it came to engaging an agent to be responsible for collecting the tolls on his behalf, Henry Grey looked further afield, to the Customs House in London where he found none other than John Whormby, the able and conscientious collector of His Majesty's customs for the port of London. It would be several years yet before Whormby became Clerk of Trinity House, but the Corporation already employed him as collector of duties for those lights which it owned. Whormby now accepted Henry Grey's invitation to act in a similar capacity for his lights at Winterton and Orford Ness.

Owing to their remote situation, neither lighthouse at Orford was intended for habitation. The front light amounted to little more than a lantern on stilts, designed to permit the sea to wash harmlessly through it during abnormal tides. The high light was more solid, being clad with timber planking or weatherboarding which afforded shelter to the keepers on watch as well as providing space where fuel and stores could be safely locked away.

On the evening of 12th April, 1720, the lights shone for the last time under Sir Edward Turnour's jurisdiction. The following morning Henry Grey arrived in Orford and called upon Sir Edward Turnour's overseer, demanding that the lighthouses be handed over. The overseer refused point blank to do so, declaring that Sir Edward had given him no instructions in the matter. Henry Grey then approached the lightkeepers, insisting that they hand over the keys. He again met with a flat refusal, whereupon he withdrew to bide his time. That evening when the keepers went over to the Ness to kindle the lights Henry Grey, accompanied by his own appointed overseer and keepers, followed them. The high lighthouse was surrounded, there was a brief scuffle and within a few moments Orford lights came under new management. [3] If Sir Edward Turnour wanted evidence to support a charge of trespass he now had it in plenty, and he immediately began his threatened lawsuit. It would be interesting to know what the outcome might have been but, on 24th June,

1721, before the matter could be brought to court, Sir Edward Turnour died and the case was not proceeded with.

The two lighthouses of which Henry Grey was now the undisputed proprietor had been neglected to a point where they were beyond repair. The high light was in a particularly dilapidated state, having withstood for eighty-three years the ravages of wind and weather and the worst assaults of the sea. Now it would have to be replaced and Henry Grey, with reckless disregard for where the money was to come from, ordered both towers to be demolished and replaced with brick ones. As John Whormby later reported:

"Both lighthouses first erected were of timber and very crazy when Mr Grey came to the patent in 1720 so that he pulled them down and built two of brick."

The new high light was built to a height of 72 feet, with a glazed lantern containing a coal fire. No description of the front light has survived apart from the information volunteered by Whormby that it was a candle lighthouse like its predecessors. The two towers together cost £1,850, a considerable sum in those days. Needless to say, the coasting trade thought it money well spent. Less enthusiastic were the mortgagors of the Morwick estate, who took the view that anyone who owed £40,000 plus accrued interest was in no position to spend nearly £2,000 on replacing lighthouses, however desperate the need.

The new front light lasted for just over three years before the continued scouring of the foreshore caused it to collapse into the sea in 1724. The plain fact was that conditions on Orford Ness made it pointless to build a strong and durable tower, necessarily immoveable and therefore doomed from the start to be overwhelmed by the uncontrollable advance of the sea. Henry Grey did not make the same mistake again. He reverted to timber for the replacement which he had built on similar lines to the front tower in use at Lowestoft. The upper portion took the form of an octagonal framework covered with overlapping boarding, and the lower portion was left unclad for the first six to eight feet above ground level so that the exposed framework would allow the sea to pass clean through with the minimum of resistance. This tower was in service by the close of the year 1724.

Henry Grey had become squire of Billingbear on the death of his brother, Grey, in 1723. As in the case of Morwick, he refused to take any part in the administration of the estate, nor could he be persuaded to plough back any of the income towards its upkeep. There is no doubt that, given time, Billingbear would have been reduced to the same state as Morwick, but as it happened, after less than three years of exploiting this latest windfall, Henry Grey was brought to an abrupt halt. By February, 1726, the interest on the Morwick loan had reached such proportions that the mortgagors foreclosed and took possession. This was a signal for Henry Grey's many other creditors to clamour for payment, giving rise to a widespread hue and cry against him.

Henry Grey reacted in dramatic fashion. He walked out of his London house carrying a pair of pistols and leaving behind two letters, one containing a message for his wife and the other addressed to a friend. In the latter Henry Grey declared his intention of committing suicide and asked the friend to go to a nominated place and recover his body. His friend hurriedly obeyed, but no trace of Henry Grey was to be found. It was later discovered that he had visited a local fishmonger who hired a stretch of salmon river from him and had collected some money due in rent, from which it was concluded that he had decided against taking his life and was planning to abscond, probably to Holland. All London became a babble of rumour and conflicting reports. Henry Grey was dead, he was alive. He was in England, he was in Holland. He was in London, he was in Berkshire. Some said that his wife was party to his disappearance and knew his whereabouts, some said that he had shot himself, but not fatally so, and was now convalescing in hiding. Others were convinced that Henry Grey had died by his own hand. Some of his servants were said to have found him with his pistols still beside him and to have carried his body home.

His continued disappearance, however, began to raise doubts in the minds of those who held him still to be alive, and the conviction began to grow that after all poor old Henry Grey had taken the easy way out. Towards the end of February Sir Robert Rich stood up in Parliament to pronounce the matter officially closed. He regretted to inform the House that, although the family were not yet prepared to admit it, Henry Grey was certainly dead.[14] This finally put paid to the uncertainty. The gossip now turned to conjecture as to how long it would be before the family acknowledged the true facts, and how they would manage to do so without losing face.

In the midst of it all Henry Grey turned up at Billingbear as if nothing had happened. Such sensational behaviour was typical of him, it kept him in the limelight. Nevertheless, the episode had a sobering effect on him. From then on his impulsive and extravagant nature began to be overshadowed by that of his more frugal and level-headed wife, who up to now had been content to remain in the background.

The marriage between Henry Grey and Elizabeth Griffin, of Dingley in Northamptonshire, brought to the Nevilles of Billingbear their most determined and dominant personality. She was the eldest daughter of James, 2nd Lord Griffin of Braybrooke, although that was rather less of a recommendation than it might appear since the family was still suffering the effects of a fall from grace on the part of Elizabeth's grandfather, the first Lord Griffin, because of his allegiance to the Catholic James II, which had resulted in Lord Griffin spending the rest of his life in the Tower and in the family being deprived of its ancient seat of Braybrooke Castle. Now, more than three generations later, they were still living in comparative seclusion. So although Elizabeth came to all intents and purposes from noble stock, nobody would have said that she was marrying beneath her station when she chose to become plain Mrs Henry Grey. She did much for the Nevilles, especially in later years when, as mistress of Billingbear, she held it within her power to control the family's destiny. For all that, Elizabeth was first and last a Griffin, whose overriding ambition was to see that family restored in wealth and honour. All her endeavours in life were devoted towards this end, and we shall see in due course how utterly successful she proved to be.

It is doubtful, however, if she ever contemplated marriage to the dunderheaded Henry Grey as a means of furthering her cause. True, it made her a member of the house of Neville, one of the leading county families of the day, but she herself would never bear that name. Nor was there any indication at that time that Henry Grey would ever succeed to Billingbear, the estate having devolved to his elder brother, Grey, who would logically bequeath it to his own heirs. As it happened Grey Neville's only daughter died an infant,

Mrs Henry Grey, later Elizabeth Countess of Portsmouth, in a portrait of about 1720.
Department of the Environment

which left Henry Grey next in line when his brother died in 1723. For Elizabeth this was an unexpected advance. It made her, at the age of thirty-two, the maternal head of the family, a position well in keeping with her inherent sense of pride and dedication. Small wonder that she now began to keep a tight rein on her frivolous and irresponsible husband, for Henry Grey, given his head, was not beyond bringing economic and social disaster on them all.

Meanwhile, out on Orford Ness, the shoreline continued to fall back in the face of the perpetual attack from the sea. In the winter of 1730-31 the front light, built six years before, was overwhelmed. A temporary light was rigged which in turn gave way to a new tower when the winter had passed. This was similar to its predecessor, but with the fundamental difference that the illuminant was now changed from candles to oil.

It was Spring, 1731. The date is significant, because it is just about the earliest instance of oil lighting superseding candles in an English lighthouse. Although this means of illumination is known to have been in domestic use throughout the Mediterranean in the twelfth century, it does not appear to have been used in a lighthouse until the lower lighthouse at Lowestoft was re-established by the Trinity Brethren in 1730 as an oil light, twenty-four years after its candle lantern had been extinguished. Henry Grey was only months behind with his light on Orford Ness. In John Whormby's survey in 1746, the only lighthouses being lit by oil were Winterton and Lowestoft, both owned by Trinity House, and Winterton Ness and Orford, owned by Henry Grey.

While waiting for the better weather to arrive, Henry Grey took the opportunity to apply for his patent to be continued when the term in being expired in 1755. This was still twenty-five years away and one wonders to what extent Henry Grey was being chivvied by the ambitious Elizabeth. This petition came before the Lords of the Treasury on 7th January, 1731, and on February 18th a Treasury Warrant was issued for an extension of thirty-six years commencing on 13th April, 1755.

The introduction of oil as a source of light brought disastrous and costly consequences. In all likelihood the keepers were unfamiliar with the properties of oil and failed to treat it with the respect it deserved, as a result of which the entire tower was burned down. It was replaced by another of similar design, again making use of timber, but this suffered the same fate as its predecessor. When, in the summer of 1732, yet another tower took its stand on Orford Ness, it was the fifth to be built there since 1720. This at least proved more successful, there was no further incidence of fire and the phase of tidal scour which had carried away four front towers in forty years appears to have come to an end. This new tower was to stand for the next sixty years.

Henry and Elizabeth Grey had no children of their own, but each had a favourite nephew within their respective families. Henry Grey was greatly attached to Richard Neville Aldworth, the son of his sister Katherine by her marriage to Richard Aldworth of Stanlake, and it was Henry Grey's expressed wish that this nephew should inherit Billingbear on condition that he changed his name from Aldworth to Neville. This changing of surnames was a common and accepted practice of the day, indulged in as a means of preserving family prestige. Henry Grey, who had himself been forced to renounce his true name for the sake of his inheritance, was now using this same lever as a way of ensuring that Billingbear would ultimately be reunited with the name of Neville. Elizabeth Grey, on the other hand, made a great favourite of John Griffin Whitwell, the eldest son of the marriage between her sister Anne and William Whitwell of Oundle. The clear indications were that this nephew would be the sole heir to all that Elizabeth already owned, or might come to own in the future, and this possibility must have caused considerable anxiety to the Nevilles. Well knowing Elizabeth's domineering disposition and powers of persuasion, they could only hope that she would not prevail upon her husband to alter his will in her favour. If this were to happen Billingbear would be certain to pass to the Griffins along with Elizabeth's other bequests.

Henry Grey was not that malleable. His will, drawn up in 1732, set out his wishes and intentions positively and rigidly. He died in September 1740, leaving his entire estate to his wife for her lifetime to hold in trust for Richard Aldworth. This will proved highly unpopular both with the Aldworths and the Nevilles, many of whom felt sure that Henry Grey intended that his nephew should benefit immediately on his death. They were convinced that he had been shaken in this resolve by the artful Elizabeth. But what else could they really expect? Henry Grey could hardly be blamed for ensuring that his widow was provided for after his death. Billingbear had been her home for the last seventeen years, and to have given it to the nephew straight away would have been to give away the roof from over her head. His wife's future wellbeing was the last thing that need have worried Henry Grey. Within a year of his death Elizabeth had remarried, had become a titled lady again and had taken a significant step up among the society of her day.

Her new husband was John Wallop, Viscount Lymington. As Viscountess Lymington, Elizabeth was now a woman of wealth and influence. She was the reigning head of the Neville family and of the Griffins, owner of Billingbear Park, principal landlord in and about Waltham St Lawrence, and patentee of the lights at Winterton and Orford Ness. Her position was further enhanced in April, 1743, when John Wallop was created 1st Earl of Portsmouth. It was in the role of Countess of Portsmouth that Elizabeth was to make her greatest impact.

In 1745 there came the greatest chance of all, when a flaw was discovered in the legal ownership of the Audley End estate, near Saffron Walden. This great country mansion, beside the main road from London to Newmarket, was built by Lord Treasurer Thomas Howard, 1st Earl of Suffolk. It was reputed to have cost £200,000 to build and was said by James I to have been "too much for a king though it might well do for a Lord Treasurer." It may have been too much for James I but it suited Charles II down to the ground, being convenient to the racing at Newmarket and more convenient still to the village of Newport, where lived the Mistress Gwynn. Audley End was acquired as a royal palace in 1669. It was returned to the Howards in 1701 and devolved from one earl to another in rapid succession until the tenth earl died, intestate, in 1745.

The legal loophole which now came to light made it appear that this line of devolution had been invalid. If this point were proven in law it would

Audley End, originally the home of the Howard family and later a royal palace of King Charles II, which eventually became the seat of the successive Lords Braybrooke. It is now in the care of the Department of the Environment.

mean that the last rightful owner had been the third earl who had died in 1688. If so, all those who had come into possession since then had done so by default. It would mean also that the only persons who now had a legitimate claim to the estate were those who could show themselves to be direct descendants of the third earl. There were only three such persons living, of whom the Countess of Portsmouth was one and her sister, Anne Whitwell, another. In 1745 the two sisters, as great-granddaughters of the third earl, joined with Lord Hervey, the remaining descendant, in laying claim to the estate. There now followed a series of protracted proceedings culminating in 1747 with Lady Portsmouth and Anne Whitwell being awarded half the estate. The house itself was excluded from the settlement because at the time of the third earl's death it was still a royal palace and could not be counted as part of his estate. To the Countess of Portsmouth this was the main prize, the home of her forebears which she was determined to regain and in which she planned to re-establish the Griffins, in surroundings befitting their former status.

Without the income from the estate the house would present a formidable financial burden. Realising this, Lady Portsmouth entered into negotiations for its outright purchase. These proceedings were brought to a successful conclusion in 1753 when the Countess became the new owner of Audley End. It was a very different Audley End from the palatial mansion which Lord Treasurer Thomas Howard had built. A succession of indifferent and transient owners had left it dilapidated and near-ruinous. The Countess of Portsmouth devoted the remainder of her life to the work of restoration, at the same time grooming her nephew and successor, John Griffin Whitwell, for the task that would one day fall to him. In anticipation of this, and conditionally upon his being made sole heir to his aunt's estate, the nephew changed his name in 1749 to John Griffin Griffin.

Lady Portsmouth died on 13th August, 1762, at the age of 71. Her death affected the Nevilles as profoundly as it did the Griffins. For more than twenty years she had presided over both families, and with the proving of her will each side at last came into its own. Audley End was left, as expected, to her nephew, John Griffin Griffin, while Billingbear passed to the other nephew, Richard Neville Aldworth, pursuant to the wishes of Henry Grey and on the condition that this nephew changed his name to Richard Neville Neville. To this extent the Countess divided the two estates fairly and evenly, duly gratifying her own wishes concerning the Griffins whilst dutifully discharging her commitments towards the Nevilles as required by the will of her late husband. There were, however, two aspects in the will which betrayed a decided bias towards the Griffins and which lead one to wonder how well the Nevilles would have fared had Lady Portsmouth been given a free hand in the disposal of Billingbear.

Firstly, there was a clause laying down that if either of the nephews died without heirs his portion would be transferred to the other nephew. This meant that if John Griffin Griffin had no children, Audley End would become the property of Richard Neville Neville. If this were to happen (as indeed it actually did) all members of the Neville family coming into possession of the estate would be required to adopt the name of Griffin. But if the reverse situation were to apply, bringing Billingbear into the hands of the Griffins, there was no proviso requiring them to take the name of Neville. From this it becomes obvious that Lady Portsmouth's only real concern was to preserve and prosper the name of Griffin and to ensure that, come what may, Audley End would henceforward be owned in that name.

The other biased point concerned the lights of Winterton and Orford Ness. Henry Grey had left these to his widow unconditionally, which meant that the Countess was free to bequeath them to whomsoever she chose. The lights had been inherited by Henry Grey in his own right, leaving no shadow of a doubt that this lucrative asset rightfully belonged to his side of the family. Despite this, Lady Portsmouth left them to John Griffin Griffin, subject to him paying the sum of £1,500 per annum out of the profits to her second husband, the Earl of Portsmouth. This represented approximately half the annual earnings of the lights at this time. When Henry Grey came to the lease in 1720 the figure had stood at £2,800 per annum.[15] In fact, the annuity was never paid, for John Wallop died on 22nd November, 1762, having survived the Countess by a mere three months.

So passed Elizabeth, Countess of Portsmouth. She had achieved in her lifetime all that she had wanted to achieve. Born into an obscure and discredited family, she had risen to become a titled lady of enormous wealth and considerable influence. Billingbear had prospered in her keeping and was now handed back to the Neville family as the seat for its future generations. She had reclaimed Audley End and had restored the name of Griffin to its former place of honour and dignity. The future of that family was now vested in her nephew and successor, John Griffin Griffin.

The new owner of Audley End and patentee of the Winterton and Orford lights had been born on 13th March, 1719, and in 1744 at the age of twenty-five he had entered the army as a commissioned officer in the foot guards. In 1758 he became a major, attaining the rank of colonel the following year and being created major-general to the forces in 1760. When he came to Audley End in 1762 it was with the rank of lieutenant-general. John Griffin Griffin immediately took up the task begun by Lady Portsmouth of restoring the mansion to its former grandeur. By the time the work was completed he was more than twenty years older and one hundred thousand pounds the poorer.

The two lighthouses on Orford Ness bequeathed by Lady Portsmouth were essentially the same as when she herself had inherited them twenty-two years before. The rear tower of the pair was the one built by her late husband in 1720, while the front tower, dating from 1732, was the one which had survived after its four predecessors had disappeared in rapid succession. Lady Portsmouth's tenure of the lease had been routine and uneventful. To her the lights were no more than a business asset, to be managed on her behalf by those retained to do so. They made a sizeable contribution to her income, but beyond that Lady Portsmouth's interest was impersonal and quite detached. She was by no means exceptional, it was the way of lighthouse owners in the eighteenth century. You erected a lighthouse and it earned you a profit. So long as that state of affairs continued, the fact that your lighthouse prevented a dozen shipwrecks or preserved a score of lives was highly satisfactory, but somewhat incidental to the main objective. And if, as often happened, it was washed down by the sea or carried away by a fall of cliff, that was rather unfortunate and you had to do something about it. But you did not normally eat into the profits by introducing costly improvements of your own accord, you waited until circumstances compelled you to do so.

Lady Portsmouth was fortunate in that nothing of the sort happened during her twenty-two years of ownership. The lease of thirty-five years granted to Henry Grey in 1720 expired in 1755, whereupon the Countess embarked upon the thirty-seven years extension which her late husband had secured in 1731. When John Griffin Griffin inherited the patent in 1762, thirty years of this second term were still to run. Needless to say, the new owner was intent on retaining possession for longer than that, so it was important that the lease was extended yet again at the earliest opportunity. What gave John Griffin Griffin real cause for concern was the changing attitude towards the concept of private lighthouse ownership. Even at this early date there were beginning to flow undercurrents of public resentment over the tremendous profits being enjoyed by a handful of privileged owners at the expense of merchant and mariner and to the detriment of navigation in general. In 1765 John Griffin Griffin judged the time ripe to present his petition, which was

Sir John Griffin Griffin, 1st Baron Bray-brooke of Braybrooke and 4th Lord Howard de Walden, owner of the lights at Winterton and Orford Ness, 1762-1797.

Department of the Environment

vigorously opposed by the Trinity Brethren but was upheld by the Lords of the Treasury, who recommended to the Privy Council that the grant should be renewed in the same terms as before.

The extended grant to Henry Grey had been calculated to produce a term of sixty-one years, from the date of his application in 1731 until 1792. In the same way Sir John Griffin Griffin's term was now made up to sixty-one years, dating from the time of his petition in 1765. Public disapproval or not, Sir John's objective was achieved. The lights of Winterton and Orford Ness were securely in the hands of himself and his successors until 1826.

The question of a successor was by now a matter requiring some consideration, since it was becoming evident that Sir John was not destined to have heirs of his own. This was the very situation catered for in the will of Lady Portsmouth, which decreed that in such circumstances Audley End would devolve to the Nevilles of Billingbear. Richard Neville Aldworth, who had been such a favourite of Henry Grey and succeeded to Billingbear following the death of Lady Portsmouth, spent most of his life abroad in the diplomatic service, in the course of which he married Magdelen Calandrini of Geneva. She had died in 1750, leaving an infant son and a daughter, and it was this son, Richard Aldworth Neville, now aged fifteen and already heir apparent to Billingbear, whom Sir John Griffin Griffin named as heir to Audley End.

In 1784 Sir John Griffin Griffin became the fourth Lord Howard de Walden. In 1788 he secured a barony, with provision for it to devolve at his death to Richard Aldworth Neville. In selecting a title for this new dignity Lord Howard sought to perpetuate the ties existing between the Griffin family and the county of Northamptonshire, choosing to become the first Lord Braybrooke of Braybrooke. The Countess of Portsmouth would have approved of that.

Throughout this time conditions on Orford Ness remained fairly static. Winters came and went, bringing the usual bout of storms with the inevitable crop of casualties at sea, but there had been no further instance of the scouring along the Ness which had proved so costly to Henry Grey earlier in the century. His low light built in 1732 still stood unmolested after more than fifty years. That run of good luck was about to come to an abrupt halt.

On the night of 31st October, 1789, there came a storm which wrought great havoc along the coast of East Anglia. At Orford Ness, it brought such drastic scouring of the shoreline that the front light was left tottering on the water's edge. There was no question of moving it further back, because it would be placed unacceptably close to the high light, and Lord Braybrooke had no option but to take the only practical course of action. A new tower was now built on the same alignment as the existing lights but set well back to the rear of the high lighthouse. When completed it stood 89 feet overall, with 163 steps leading to the lantern, which was lit by oil, with fourteen lamps set in silver-plated reflectors. The new lighthouse came into service on the night of 6th May, 1793. Between it and the front tower stood the former high lighthouse, temporarily out of use but destined for conversion to the role of front light using oil in place of the coal fire. It was brought back into service on the night of 14th October, 1793, whereupon the old front light was abandoned to the sea.

The eve of All Hallows, 1789, had been a costly one for Lord Braybrooke, both here and at Winterton. Exactly how costly is not known, but the expense

Orford Ness lighthouse about 1914, with keepers' houses on both sides of the tower. These houses have now been removed, as can be seen from the picture on page 53.

incurred was still being seized upon by Lord Braybrooke's successor many years later as justification for a further extension of the lease.

Lord Braybrooke died on 25th May, 1797, aged 78 and was laid among the Howards in the family vault at Saffron Walden. Richard Aldworth Neville, who now became the 2nd Lord Braybrooke, did not have as much enthusiasm for Audley End as John Griffin Griffin, though that is not to say that he neglected the place. The plain fact was that the second Lord Braybrooke was a Neville, and the Nevilles were of Billingbear. He did not, as the first lord had done, move his family seat to Audley End. To him the traditional red-brick manor of Billingbear, in its natural setting of parkland, held more appeal than the ornate stonework of Audley End and the still unmellowed landscaping of "Capability" Brown. Consequently the second Lord Braybrooke undertook no ambitious schemes for the embellishment of the house or the beautification of its grounds, as his predecessor had done and as his own son would do in the future.

Richard Aldworth Neville had been born at Stanlake, close to Billingbear, in 1750. Embarking at the age of twenty-four upon a career in public and political life, he was currently Member for Reading and also High Steward of Wokingham, a dignity at one time enjoyed by Henry Grey. He married Catherine, youngest daughter of the Honourable George Grenville, in June, 1780, and succeeded to Billingbear in 1793 on the death of his father, Richard Neville Neville. His wife died in 1797 shortly before the first Lord Braybrooke, and so did not live to see her husband come into the Audley End inheritance. That inheritance marked not only the transfer of the Griffin estates to the Nevilles, it brought the ownership of the lights to Billingbear, as Henry Grey would always have wished.

Unlike previous owners, the second Lord Braybrooke did not take the opportunity of ensuring an extension of the lease far in advance of its termination, an unwise omission in view of the mounting opposition to private enterprise in lighthouses. The current extension, secured by the first Lord Braybrooke, had not been easily come by, and the more time that passed the less favourable became the chances of obtaining a further grant, chances rendered slimmer still by the proposal by the Select Committee on Foreign Trade that no further private leases should be issued, and all existing grants should become the property of Trinity House upon the expiration of their terms in being. In 1824, with only two years of his lease remaining and despite the Select Committee's categorical recommendations, Lord Braybrooke petitioned for a renewal of his patent. This was justified, he argued, on the grounds that he had not had sufficient time to recoup the expense of improving and rebuilding his towers at Orford Ness and Winterton.

He, in fact, had suffered no expense at all. The cost had been borne by the first Lord Braybrooke, and there were probably those who felt that anyone who could afford to spend one hundred thousand pounds on restoring his home could well afford to spend a few hundreds more in the cause of humanity. Others may have thought that there had already been ample time to recover expenses that had been incurred thirty-five years previously. Objections such as these, strengthened by the findings of the Select Committee, and the more authoritative voice with which Trinity House now spoke, all combined to make Lord Braybrooke's case the more difficult to sustain. Such proceedings are necessarily protracted, however, and before the

Richard Neville Neville, 3rd Lord Braybrooke of Braybrooke (1783-1858), the last
private owner of the Orford Ness lights.
*Department of the Environment (by kind
permission of the Hon Robin Neville)*

matter could be resolved Lord Braybrooke died at Billingbear on 28th
February, 1825. He was buried in the church at Waltham St Lawrence with
other members of the Neville family.

The Honourable Richard Neville, who now succeeded as the third Lord
Braybrooke, took after the first lord more than the second, in that his heart
and soul were in Audley End. But whereas the first lord had concentrated his
attention on the exterior of the house and its grounds, the new owner devoted
his efforts to the inside. Richard Neville was born in 1783, the third son of the
marriage between the second Lord Braybrooke and Lady Catherine. He grew
up a man of many interests, with a good head for business, a keen interest in
politics and a flair for writing and historical research. He sat in Parliament for
Thirsk and Saltash before taking over his father's former constituency of
Buckingham, and also followed him into what had now become a traditional
family appointment, that of High Steward of Wokingham. On 13th May,
1819, he married the Lady Jane Cornwallis, eldest daughter of the second
Marquis Cornwallis of Brome Hall in Suffolk.

It was the third Lord Braybrooke who, as all the world knows, edited and
prepared for publication the original edition of Samuel Pepys's diary. His
editing was, to say the least, drastic. The finished work, published under the
title of *Memoirs of Samuel Pepys Esq. F.R.S.*, really amounted to a volume of
selected passages from the diary. Pepys took every opportunity to record his

stern disapproval of the whole system of private lighthouse ownership. His most forthright comments are found among his Naval Minutes, but the Diary does contain a number of entries having a bearing on the subject. One of them announces the successful outcome of a particular private application and predicts a source of rich profit for the fortunate owner, and on another occasion Pepys records being approached by a would-be patentee with the offer of one hundred pounds in return for his assistance in furthering the project.[16] These and similar entries are omitted from Lord Braybrooke's original edition. With the petition for an extension of his own lease currently under consideration, and receiving a rough passage into the bargain, did Lord Braybrooke perhaps conclude that the less Samuel Pepys had to say about lighthouses at this inopportune time the better?

When he succeeded to the title, the new heir soon let it be known that he was as intent on procuring a renewal as his father. He had little success in speeding matters up and for the next three years the proposal was tossed back and forth between the Treasury Office and Trinity House. It was early in 1828

The Orford Ness lights in 1834, from a picture by Clarkson Stanfield. The tower in the foreground is that built by Henry Grey in 1720; having outlasted five front towers it is seen here acting as the front light to the tower in the distance which still survives today. In the far distance can be seen the masts of ships lying in the River Ore.

before the long-awaited verdict was made known. The grant was renewed for a term of twenty-five years from 1st June, 1824, the date of the second Lord Braybrooke's application, but was subject to much more drastic conditions than in the past.

Investigations had revealed that over the preceding three years the average profits from the two sets of lights amounted to £13,414 per annum with all expenses met. The new grant slashed the rate of tolls from one penny to one halfpenny per ton. Additionally half the profits would in future be claimed by the Crown. Effectively, then, the revenue accruing to Lord Braybrooke would be reduced to one quarter of what it had previously been, yet the decision was not well received, by the coasting trade, Trinity House, or for that matter, the world at large. In fact this lease was terminated after less than nine years by the Act of Parliament passed in 1836. Two years earlier the Committee for Trade had protested that there could be no justification for the continued favour being shown to Lord Braybrooke. His lordship must have already realised that there was little hope of renewing his lease beyond the current term and with the passing of the Act he promptly settled for the prescribed rate of compensation, the lights being taken over by Trinity House on 1st January, 1837.

Two improvements were immediately introduced in the vicinity of Orford. Firstly, a floating light was established at the Shipwash Sand, nearly eight miles south-east of Orford.[17] A lightvessel is still on this station today and is visible to the naked eye from the top of Orford Castle. Secondly, a new lens of French design was installed at the Low Lighthouse in January, 1838. Later that year two additional burners were fitted to the High Lighthouse, bringing the total there to sixteen.

In 1887, for the first time in many years, a tremendous storm caused drastic scouring of the foreshore. Near Butley Creek the sea breached the shingle bank, bursting through to the river beyond and flooding the adjoining marshes. As on so many occasions in the past, the Low Lighthouse was left standing precariously at the water's edge, and within a short time it had gone the way of its eight predecessors. That was the end of front towers on Orford Ness, Trinity House deciding instead to establish a new lighthouse altogether at a point further up the coast where it would be more easily seen by shipping approaching from the north.

Beyond Orford the next salient point of the coast is at Southwold which, due to the trend of the land, lies nearly four miles further east than the easternmost point of Orford Ness. In this region of low coast and flat marshes, high ground is a relative feature, so that Southwold, standing on a modest slope of rising ground, enjoys a commanding view across an extensive seascape. Here was an ideal location for the new lighthouse and a search began for a suitable site. Meanwhile, owing to the desperate plight of the front

The temporary light which stood on Southwold Denes, between the town and the harbour entrance, throughout the two years that the permanent lighthouse in the town was under construction. *Southwold Museum*

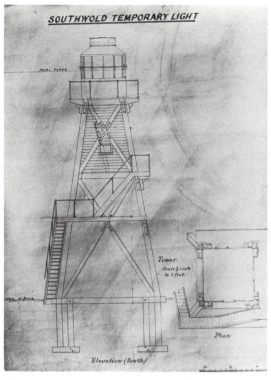

SOUTHWOLD TEMPORARY LIGHT

Tower
Scale ¼ inch
to 1 foot.

Plan

Elevation (South)

lighthouse at Orford, a temporary light was set up on Southwold denes a short distance north of the harbour entrance. This structure incorporated a conventional lantern, carried aloft on a trelliswork of stout timber.

The site eventually chosen for the permanent lighthouse was the highest spot in Southwold, at the junction of East Green and what was then St James Street, now Stradbroke Road. Building began late in 1887 under the supervision of Mr James Walker, Engineer-in-Chief to Trinity House and builder of Hunstanton and Cromer towers, among others. The completed tower was carried to a height of 101 feet overall, making it 120 feet from sea level to the focus of the light. The new lighthouse was lit for the first time on the night of 19th February, 1889, displaying a white occulting light over a distance of 17 miles. An occulting light is one in which the period of light is sustained for longer than the succeeding interval of darkness, making it the opposite of a flashing light. In the case of Southwold the character allotted was fourteen seconds light, two seconds dark, two seconds light and two seconds dark, giving an overall sequence of 20 seconds.

Occulting lights are less common now than in the days of oil or gas lighting, when a flashing character was less easy to achieve. Since the light

itself could not be extinguished and rekindled in rapid succession, any interruption had to be effected by means of a screen or hood momentarily obscuring the light. With electrification it became possible to produce a flashing character by switching the light on and off at source, and many occulting lights were replaced by flashing ones as the programme of electrification progressed. Southwold lighthouse was electrified and first shone as a flashing light on 23rd February, 1938.

Such were the circumstances which brought Southwold lighthouse into being in the early days of 1889. With it there disappeared from the Orford scene the tower built by Henry Grey which had stood as a seamark for 170 years. It had witnessed the destruction of no fewer than five front towers, two by fire and three by the advance of the sea. The remaining lighthouse at Orford now assumed the status of a major coastwise light. Owing to its remote and inaccessible situation it was classed as a rock station, with a complement of three keepers and with no families permitted to live on the premises. By 1908 Orford light had been converted to incandescant gas, producing a light of 35,000 candle-power.

During and after the First World War, Orford Ness was put to increasing military use.* In 1934 it was made a restricted area and has remained so ever

*See *Orfordness, Secret Site,* by Gordon Kinsey (Terence Dalton, 1981).

84

since. With the electrification of the lighthouse shortly after the Second World War, the keepers were withdrawn and the station became automatic. Throughout the war years strange and secret things took place on Orford Ness. It was here that the first experiments were conducted in the use of radio direction finding, while at nearby Bawdsey Manor there was established the first of Britain's operational radar stations. Ironically, Orford lighthouse stood silent witness to the birth of these revolutionary beams which were soon to relegate it and all others of its kind to a role of secondary importance. Since the war Orford Ness has remained under strict military control, with access forbidden to all unauthorised persons. During these years the lighthouse has continued in service without interruption. Boldly striped in red and white, it stands aloof on the furthermost point of the Ness, its white light flashing at five-second intervals.

Nearly two centuries have passed since John Griffin Griffin built Orford tower. With the exception of Happisburgh, which dates from 1791, Orford is the oldest lighthouse on the east coast. When first built it was separated from the front lighthouse by a distance of 1,439 yards. Today the sea is perhaps 200 yards from it. That may seem a respectable distance, but to the North Sea, which has, in the past, removed 400 yards of cliff in a single night and has swallowed villages in a matter of years, two hundred yards of loose, unstable shingle is a slender barrier indeed.

CHAPTER FOUR

Lowestoft

To the furthermost horizon throw your light,
With vivid ray the homing sailor greet,
"Fear not, good sailor, fear you not the night,
A welcome here awaits you at my feet."
(*Ode to a Lighthouse* — Stuart Neville)

I N COMMON with neighbouring Norfolk and the shores of Holderness, the
Suffolk coast is soft and easily eroded. Powerful tides sweep it with perpetual
and clockwork regularity, grading its beaches from expanses of fine sand in the
north to ridges of coarse shingle in the south. Where cliffs occur they are of a
loose gravel-like consistency, offering little in the way of resistance to wave
erosion.

Time and tide have left their mark on the Suffolk coast, smoothing away
its headlands and silting up its indentations, giving the county a more
straightforward outline than in days gone by. Beyond the present-day tideline
lie several hamlets and at least one sizeable town, all claimed by the sea within
the span of a few centuries. Due to the scouring effects of the longshore drift
the coast of East Anglia remains in a state of continual transition. Material
which the sea eats away at one point, it regurgitates at another, land fading
from one place to reappear elsewhere in the form of a shingle spit. The sea,
having gnawed for centuries at a particular cliff-line, may all at once relent
and begin to lay a protective coating of sand beneath the cliffs, as if it would
dress the wounds it has inflicted.

This is especially evident at Lowestoft, where a wide tract of sand and
marram grass fringes the base of an ancient cliff to form the area known as
The Beach. Lowestoft's role as a fishing centre had its origins on this
foreshore, whose inhabitants considered themselves a community apart and
spoke of "going to Lowestoft" whenever they ascended the steep paths, or
scores, to the upper part of the town.

Out to sea a line of sandbanks running parallel with the coast creates a
continuation of the Roads which are of such paramount importance to
Yarmouth. One fact revealed by Greenville Collins' survey of 1685 was that

Lowestoft high light, Britain's most easterly
light.   *D. J. Leech*

these sands were in reality one vast bank, connected by extensive areas which remained submerged at all states of the tide. The main fairway into Lowestoft Roads lay through a gap between the Holme Bank and the Bernard Sand, a narrow and tortuous approach known as the Standforth Channel. In the course of time this name became corrupted to Stanford and the Bernard Sand became the Barnard.

The first reliable survey of Suffolk was that undertaken by Christopher Saxton in 1575. The resulting map showed the coast to be dominated by Easton Ness, which constituted at that time the most salient point on the east coast. Like its counterpart at Winterton, this promontory suffered extensively over the years from erosion, and to the less-prominent Lowestoft Ness fell the distinction of becoming the most easterly point of the British Isles. For the greater part of three centuries Lowestoft Ness was itself subjected to severe tidal scour, until in 1903 the construction of a concrete sea wall between Pakefield Cliffs and the North Denes finally brought the process to a halt.

*   *   *   *   *   *

It was stated in sworn evidence heard by the board of enquiry into the Winterton dispute in 1621 that the original lights at Caister and Lowestoft were erected by a private individual named Bushell at his own cost and charges. This venture was successfully opposed by the Trinity Brethren and Bushell was obliged to take from them a lease of twenty-one years at an annual rental of sixty pounds.[1] Whether or not this lease ran its full term is uncertain, but in 1600 the Brethren assumed responsibility for the Caister lights and in 1609 they similarly took over Lowestoft. The fact that there is no record of them obtaining a patent to do so supports the contention that they already held the grant which they had hitherto leased to Bushell.

They now erected a pair of leading lights, the usual structures of latticed timber supporting candle lanterns, on the low-lying foreshore at Lowestoft Ness. The towers stood in a line marking the deepest water of the Stanford Channel, and in return for their services dues were payable at the rate of twelve-pence per hundred tons on ships of burden, and fourpence per voyage for fishing craft. By 1628 the lighthouses were found to be in a bad state of repair and were rebuilt in similar form. The new towers managed to survive for close on another fifty years, at the end of which time it was again necessary to rebuild.

There were various reasons for this, some more obvious than others. Firstly, the lighthouses had become hemmed in by the building of fishermen's huts and dwellings nearby, causing the lights to be partially obscured, and secondly the role of the station had changed somewhat during the sixty years since it first came into service. The lights had come to be relied upon not only by vessels feeling their way cautiously along the coast, but by those approaching from far out to sea. As John Whormby later explained:

> "When first established they were only for the direction of ships which crept by night in the dangerous passage between Lowestoft and Winterton, through channels which lay close under the shore; although later found to be of further use to ships crossing the sea, yet that was not their original design."

Not for the first time along this coast a local inshore mark had graduated to the status of a major navigational beacon. Clearly the situation called for something brighter and more reliable than the flickering candles which had served for so long at Lowestoft. These were the more obvious and plausible reasons which prompted Trinity House to introduce improvements.

But in all truth there were more subtle and compelling motives which they did less to publicise. A few months previously a new light had shone out over Yarmouth Roads. After seven years of legal wrangling, the persistent John Clayton had at last contrived to kindle his light at Corton, three miles up the coast. This took the form of a coal light displayed from the top of a structure which a contemporary writer described as "the most curious lighthouse in Christendom". It would be easy to misconstrue what this writer was really trying to say. Nowadays we regard as curious anything that is in any way peculiar or a trifle odd. In former times, however, the word described something that was remarkable or worthy of note. Daniel Defoe, for instance, set out on his tour through eastern England in search of "whatever is curious and worth Observation." This description was, therefore, a compliment to, rather than a criticism of, John Clayton's light.

Clayton, who up to now had been a mere thorn in the flesh, was beginning to emerge as a real and serious threat to the monopoly of the Trinity Brethren, who immediately set about finding means of retaliation. The only sure way was for them to make their lights at Lowestoft more effective than Clayton's light at Corton, and therein lay the true reason behind the decision to improve the Lowestoft lights.

On Trinity Monday of this year 1676, in accordance with their annual custom, the Brethren of Trinity House foregathered at Deptford Strond to elect one from their number who would serve as Master throughout the ensuing twelve-month term. Their choice on this occasion lay with one who was to prove himself one of the most capable and purposeful Masters ever to preside over their affairs, Mr Samuel Pepys. It seems strange that the world at large should never cease to be fascinated by Samuel Pepys the Diarist, or be indulgently amused by Samuel Pepys the Philanderer, yet should remain coolly indifferent to the accomplishments of Samuel Pepys, Member of Parliament and Justice of the Peace, Samuel Pepys, President of the Royal

Society and Principal Officer of the Navy Board, or Samuel Pepys, Elder Brother and twice Master of Trinity House and Secretary of the Admiralty of England.

This mastery of naval matters, this relish for maritime affairs, is a part of the Pepys character which his background and environment do little to explain. He came from no long line of distinguished or venturesome seafarers, nor was his education intended in any way to fit him for a career concerned with the sea. Samuel Pepys was schooled in the Fens where he became conditioned more to the stagnant stench of swamp and marsh than to the tang of salt air in his nostrils. It was through his cousin, Lord Montague, that Pepys became associated with the Navy. At the Restoration, in the general clamour for positions of favour and high office, Montague secured for Pepys the post of Clerk of the Acts of the Navy, thereby setting him off on a career which was to reward him with power, authority and social standing. For Samuel Pepys this was a fortunate day; it was an equally fortunate one for England.

Pepys realised that his country's future depended on the virility of her seaborne trade and the strength of her fighting ships. He was ever critical of

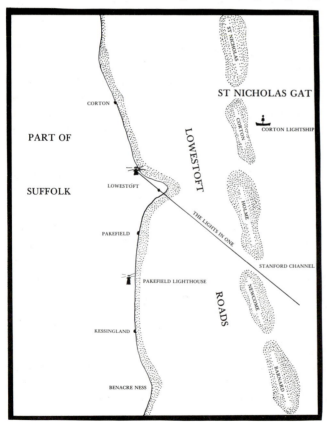

his fellow countrymen's disregard of this, a trait which, as he once pointed out, was even reflected in their choice of a patron saint:

> "England has taken a knight errant, Saint George, for its guardian saint, and not any of the Apostles and other fishermen that would have had more relation to the sea."

Long before Charles II commanded a survey to be taken of our coastal waters, Pepys was urging Trinity House to take upon itself the task of sounding and charting the approaches to our shores. It was at Pepys' suggestion that Captain Greenville Collins was made a Younger Brother, and at his instigation Trinity House donated the sum of fifty pounds, that it might be publicly associated with the project.

In his capacity of Clerk of the Acts, Pepys soon found that additional sources of income were readily come by. If from his Diary it becomes obvious that he was not beyond accepting the occasional bribe or piece of silver plate, it should be realised that he was by no means alone in this. Bribery seemed to be taken for granted throughout the administration of the Navy and it stands to Pepys' credit that he indulged in it far less than most. "But Good God," he once remarked, "What a man might do were I a knave." [2]

But if Samuel Pepys be guilty of a measure of malpractice in his transactions on behalf of the Navy, it is a charge that can scarcely be repeated in respect of his associations with Trinity House. From the day in 1662 when he was first elected a Younger Brother he put the rights and interests of the Corporation before all else. In the matter of coast lights especially he took the firmest of stands. He was resolutely opposed to them being erected by private enterprise and he roundly condemned all those who sought to do so:

> "Observe the evil of having lights raised by, and for the profit of private men, and not for the good of the public or the relief of poor seamen." [3]

It was his unswerving allegiance to Trinity House which ultimately cost Pepys his seat in Parliament. [4] In both these maritime fields Pepys quickly rose to prominence. In 1673 he was appointed Secretary to the Admiralty, a post which gave him a large say in shaping naval policy. Now, in 1676, he found himself elected to the Mastership of Trinity House for the first of two terms which he was to serve.

Pepys lost no time in coming to grips with the situation at Lowestoft. Presiding over one of his first meetings of the Trinity House Court, he ordered:

> "Let it be seen whether Sir John Clayton's grant can be stopped before passing the Great Seal, until such time as some Gentlemen of this House can go down to inspect the lights at Leystaffe, and then a Report will be given in to the Lords of the Council concerning the Lights at Corton." [5]

The "gentlemen" referred to were in reality Captain Hugh Till and Mr Simon Bailey, together with Sir Thomas Allin, who were also concerned together in the building of the Small Light at Winterton. The result of their visit to Lowestoft was made known to a meeting of the Court at Trinity House on 26th June, 1676. They recommended that the lights should continue to indicate a safe approach through the Stanford Channel, but that the high light should be rebuilt to serve additionally as a major coastwise light. It should take the form of a tower lighthouse lit by a coal fire, and in order that it might be more easily seen by ships at a distance, it should be located on the ridge of the former cliff along which the town of Lowestoft was steadily expanding. This proposal brought strong objections from one of the Elder Brethren, Captain Crisp, who maintained that both of the lights should be built on this ridge. Captain Till replied that all the shipmasters thereabouts had been consulted and all were agreed that "one should be above and the other below."

Samuel Pepys directed that before a decision was finally taken, the report should be referred back to Sir Thomas Allin for his further observations. Sir Thomas replied by letter from Somerleyton Hall on 7th July, saying that he still agreed with the original proposal. Three days later he again wrote to say that he had revisited the site and enclosed a certificate signed by several local shipmasters and fishermen stating their agreement to the lights being set up as proposed.

By the end of August plans were finalised. Sir Thomas Allin was requested to obtain brick, stone and oak timber for the floors. Building commenced early in September and by mid-October the Trinity Brethren were able to make the following announcement:

NOTICE TO MARINERS

"The Master, Wardens and Assistants of the Trinity House of Deptford Strond, finding on a survey lately by them taken of their two ancient lighthouses at Leystaffe upon the Coast of Suffolk that the upper of the said Lights is by the too near approach of certain dwelling houses lately erected there rendered less easie to be distinguished than here-to-fore have (for the benefit of Navigation trading alongst that Coast, at their own proper Cost and Charges, and without any increase of Duty to be expected for the same) removed the said upper Lighthouse to a Hill somewhat more distant to the northward thereof and converted the same from a Candle to a Fire Light, moving also the lower Light so as to be S.S.E. from the upper, effectually serving for the directing ships safe through the Stamford Channel and clear of the Holme Head; which Lights so placed, being forthwith to be kindled Publick Notice is hereby given thereof."[6]

Throughout the rebuilding Samuel Pepys maintained a keen and active

The upper lighthouse at Lowestoft, built in 1676 under the direction of Samuel Pepys, as it appeared in 1812.

Suffolk County Library, Lowestoft

interest. He obviously derived a great deal of satisfaction from the fact that the new tower had been erected during his period of office. Now that it was completed he arranged for a plaque of carved stone to be affixed to the lighthouse. In the upper portion was displayed the coat-of-arms of the Corporation of Trinity House, and in the lower field appeared the two nags' heads and fleurs-de-lis of the Pepyses of Cottenham. This plaque was fixed outside the entrance to the tower, where it remained throughout the life of the lighthouse. When the building was eventually demolished almost two centuries later, the plaque was preserved and after being renovated was erected in the tower of the present lighthouse where it remains to this day.

The two Elder Brethren who had been responsible for the building of the new lighthouse, Captain Till and Mr Bailey, were each rewarded for their services. Captain Till received a piece of silver plate and Mr Bailey a sum of money. Two years later, having successfully completed the Small Light at

Winterton, they both went to the Isles of Scilly and built St Agnes lighthouse there.

The decision to insist on the new light being located on top of the ridge proved to be a sound one. In this more elevated position the lighthouse assumed the status of a major coastwise light in addition to its role in

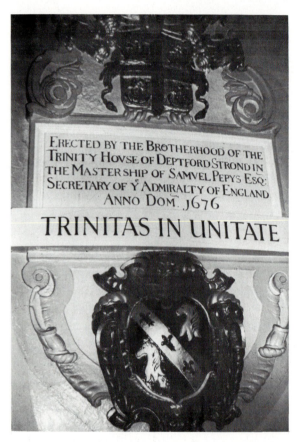

ERECTED BY THE BROTHERHOOD OF THE TRINITY HOVSE OF DEPTFORD STROND IN THE MASTERSHIP OF SAMVEL PEPYS ESQ: SECRETARY OF Ỹ ADMIRALTY OF ENGLAND ANNO DOM: 1676

TRINITAS IN UNITATE

The plaque containing the Pepys arms preserved in the tower of the present Lowestoft lighthouse.

association with the low light. It was now visible to ships for many miles up and down the coast and was, in all respects, as efficient and useful as Clayton's light at Corton.

But if the sailors rejoiced in the improvements effected at Lowestoft, the population of the town had the gravest misgivings. The events of a night only six years before were all too fresh in their memories. A fire had started in the tightly-packed confines of the town, reducing dozens of dwellings to smouldering shells. Twenty-four years before that, a similar tragedy had occurred when fire broke out in the long and narrow sheds down by the

Ropewalk; sheds of timber coated with pitch, and filled to capacity with the wooden barrels in which the herring were salted down. That night had cost ten thousand pounds in damage, and when the flames at last died away more than 140 houses lay in ruins. The town had grown considerably since then and another large fire would be little short of catastrophic; yet here was Samuel Pepys's tower belching smoke and cascading sparks high over the roof-tops. The Trinity Brethren listened sympathetically to the appeal put before them, and early the next year Captain Till returned to Lowestoft to supervise the building of a lantern to enclose the fire. It was glazed in with 324 panes of best crown glass, and the townsfolk slept easier in their beds.

On first hearing of the Trinity Brethren's intention to rebuild their Lowestoft lights Sir John Clayton lodged an immediate objection. It would, he protested, be detrimental to his interests at Corton, and he recalled that Trinity House had long ago certified that there was no further need of lights on the coasts of England. Since the proposal involved the replacement of two existing lights, rather than the establishment of a new one, his argument was hardly valid. By an Order-in-Council dated 9th August, 1676, Charles II directed the Committee for Trade to intervene in the dispute between Sir John Clayton and the Trinity House over their light on the cliff at Lowestoft.[7]

Clayton then complained to the King that although the lighthouses granted to himself and George Blake were all built, owing to constant objections only the one at St Nicholas Gat had been lit. The tolls for it were not paid according to expectation because the dues had been determined as an inclusive figure to cover all his proposed lights; no specific rate had been fixed for any single lighthouse. As a result authority was given for Sir John Clayton (the said Blake being dead) to receive ¼d per ton on English and ½d per ton on "stranger" ships passing any of the said lighthouses "when burning, in respect of each one so burning."[8]

Even this did not avail Clayton to any extent, for the only light burning so far was the one at Corton, and the income from that alone would hardly be sufficient to finance the building and commissioning of the other three. Sir John Clayton at last came to realise that he was fighting a losing battle. He now approached the Trinity Brethren, offering to pay them one hundred pounds a year if they would support his venture at Corton. But having been put to the trouble and expense of altering their lights at Lowestoft, the Brethren were naturally in no mood to strike bargains. Clayton then offered them the sum of five hundred pounds a year to withdraw their opposition to all his projects, but this also produced a firm refusal. By 1678 Clayton was in desperate straits. His grant had stipulated that the specified tolls were to be voluntary, and up to now his light at St Nicholas Gat had yielded only sixty pounds.

Once again Clayton petitioned the King, explaining that although he had spent £3,000 on the building of his various lighthouses, he was not able to derive any benefit from them on account of some legal defect in the wording of the Letters Patent. He therefore prayed that His Majesty would accept a surrender of the grant and favour him instead with a patent for Corton only, the dues and rent to be as before. To this the King gave consent and renewed the grant on those terms, the Letters Patent being dated 23rd January, 1677-78.

It began to look as if John Clayton had at last succeeded in his aspirations to become the proprietor of a lighthouse. But the Trinity Brethren still had a trump card up their sleeve which they now chose to play. For an unspecified period they declared the Lowestoft lights free of all tolls. It was the straw which very quickly broke John Clayton's back. Many had been in favour of his light when he had first kindled it and had pledged their contined patronage, but now that a new light had appeared only a stone's throw away, fulfilling all the advantages of the light at Corton, and for which no payment was being asked, support for Clayton's project dwindled rapidly. In little more than a year his tower at Corton stood abandoned. It was not quite the end of the Corton story, nor was it the last the Trinity Brethren ever heard of Sir John Clayton. In 1680 they clashed with him again when he contested their proposal to erect St Agnes lighthouse. As it happened Clayton's counter-claim came a little late; the grant was already signed and sealed in the Corporation's favour.

Apparently Clayton managed to dispose of his interests at Corton to one Henry Bowyer, to whom Letters Patent were issued in July, 1682, authorising him to maintain a double light at Corton.[9] Presumably Bowyer was intending to operate a pair of leading lights to indicate the entrance to St Nicholas Gat, using Clayton's existing tower as one of the pair. Although the grant was confirmed again a few months later, nothing ever came of it in practice, so it can only be assumed that Henry Bowyer fared no better than Sir John Clayton in his endeavours at Corton. The final word of all fell to Samuel Pepys, who was collecting material for his projected history of the Navy. He made a note reminding himself to make mention of Corton Light, "which burned for about a year and a half circa. 1679."[10]

Unlike most privately-owned lights, where it was left to the agent to hire the keepers and pay them from his overall allowance, Trinity House employed its own keepers, who were directly on the pay-roll. In consequence records of successive keepers are more intact here than at any of the other lighthouses featured in this book. There is an entry for Michaelmas, 1682, relating that one of the keepers, a man by the name of John George, had neglected his duty. He was replaced by George Prince at a salary of £26 per annum, which was raised to £30 after he had completed a year's satisfactory service.

Despite the fact that the high light had been placed in a more prominent position, it was not long before new buildings being erected in the vicinity partially obscured the light from certain directions out to sea. Trinity House conducted an offshore survey in 1688 and as a result of the findings the tower was heightened by ten feet.

In 1706 the low light down on the foreshore was, suddenly and without warning, discontinued. It can only be surmised that the sea overwhelmed it, and that no replacement was provided. For many years after, complaints were continually made of the difficulty experienced in navigating the Stanford Channel. Eventually, in 1730 a new low light which took the form of a timber structure of weather-boarding surmounted by a lantern displaying the light from three open-flame oil burners was brought into service. The entire

The old timber low light at Lowestoft, moved along the beach from time to time to keep pace with the changing Stanford Channel.

lighthouse was designed to be easily moved so that it could be kept in alignment with the fairway, which was subject to unpredictable change due to tidal scour.

It was reported at this time that the overseer, a man by the name of Wilde, had been neglectful of his duties. Further enquiries revealed that he did not even live locally and his services were dispensed with.

The first change in the position of the low light became necessary in 1735, due to a sudden shift in the course of the Stanford Channel. Such changes were, of course, brought about by the upheaving of the outer sands, usually occurring with the onset of the winter storms, which appear by local records to have been consistently severe during the month of December. The storm of Christmas Eve, 1739, was a typical example, when tremendous seas engulfed the once proud port of Dunwich and sixteen ships were driven ashore between

Yarmouth and Lowestoft. On 15th December, 1757, a further twenty-two ships were wrecked off Lowestoft, while in December, 1770, one of the worst storms of all took place. On the section of coast between Yarmouth and Southwold, thirty ships and two hundred lives were lost. First light next day revealed eighteen vessels cast up on Lowestoft beach, and by nine o'clock that morning more than a dozen had broken up.[11]

On the death of Samuel Harris, who had served as overseer for nearly twenty years, the Trinity Brethren appointed Henry Bolson, "a man of Honesty, Fidelity and Diligence" at the usual salary of £35 per annum.

There are in existence several engravings and paintings which illustrate the lighthouses at Lowestoft as they were at this time. Included in these are works by J. M. W. Turner, an artist perhaps more generally associated with sunsets and sky effects. In fact Turner painted anything and everything, and water and shipping feature plentifully in his works. Another interesting illustrative source is found in the products of the famous Lowestoft porcelain factory, in particular in the work of one of its leading decorative painters, Richard Powles. He became one of the most skilled and prolific of the many

decorative painters known to have worked at the factory, and it is his work which adorns many of the finest pieces of Lowestoft porcelain to be found today.

A favourite view of his, found in much of his work, was that from the North Battery, with the high lighthouse in the foreground and the low lighthouse in the distance on the shoreline. Nowhere does this occur in more minute and colourful detail than upon a commemoration mug now in the Castle Museum in Norwich. The scene is surmounted by the coat-of-arms of Trinity House, with the upper and lower lighthouses depicted in great detail. An identical mug is in the Victoria and Albert Museum at South Kensington. Almost certainly there were others, all produced as presentation pieces to mark the installation of a new lighting apparatus at the upper lighthouse in 1778. The mug at Norwich is said to have been presented to Mr Davey, who is described as being the superintendent of the lighthouse. To be more accurate, William Davies, who lived at Yarmouth, was the agent for Trinity House in this district, with responsibility for the lights at Caister and the Small Light at Winterton as well as those at Lowestoft. As such he would have been a prime

Opposite: A drawing of the Lowestoft high light by Richard Powles, probably showing it as it was before the rebuilding of the top of the tower to receive the new "spangle light."
Suffolk County Library, Lowestoft

Right: A commemorative mug made at the Lowestoft porcelain factory and decorated by Richard Powles. It is said to have been presented to William Davies, the Trinity House agent at Yarmouth, to mark the installation of the "spangle light" in 1778.
Norfolk Museums Service, Norwich Castle Museum

candidate to receive a commemorative piece of porcelain, as would the distinguished party of Elder Brethren who arrived at Lowestoft on 23rd June, 1778, to view the new apparatus set up on a temporary scaffolding in readiness for a trial by comparison with the high lighthouse that evening.

The new mechanism consisted basically of a large drum, coated on the outside with hundreds of small squares of silvered glass. The whole was encircled by a fixed pipe containing oil, into which was set a total of 126 lamp

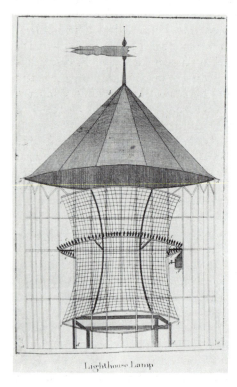

Lighthouse Lamp

The "spangle light" installed at Lowestoft high light in 1778. The concave surface of the central drum was coated with 4,000 small squares of mirror glass which reflected the light from 126 lamp wicks set in the surrounding oil feed pipe.

Norfolk Museums Service

wicks. The circle of dancing flames was reflected in the mirrors and projected far and wide. Much the same idea can be seen today in shop windows, when a mirror-encrusted turntable sparkles in the light from the window lamps as it revolves to display the goods set out on it. Another modern adaptation is the silvered globe suspended high in the roof of a dance hall, sending pin points of concentrated light in all directions as it turns in the glare of a spotlight.

Having inspected this machine at close quarters, the visiting party embarked in the Trinity House yacht and sailed far out to sea so as to be at as great a distance as possible by nightfall. As darkness gathered the yacht set course for the shore when, to the great satisfaction of all on board, the new light became visible at a range of more than twenty miles. The yacht had to sail another five or six miles before the coal fire at the high lighthouse could be seen.[12] The next day the prototype apparatus was dismantled and the Trinity Brethren sailed off in their yacht, well pleased with the results of their experiment.

In the event the new invention proved to be less efficient than had at first been supposed. It has since been described as the "spangle light"[13] and it would be hard to think of a more fitting name. The best that could be said for it was that it glittered. Whilst the reflecting surfaces achieved the object of diverting the light-rays towards the direction required, they lacked the scientific shape necessary to concentrate those rays into a narrow beam. The result was that much of the total intensity was lost through light scatter. One or two of these machines were retained in service for a limited period, that at Lowestoft lasting for about eighteen years, but the system perfected by Mr Walker of Lynn* coupled with the invention of a revolutionary oil burner by the Swiss engineer Amie Argand quickly rendered these spangle lights obsolete.

The abolition of the fire light robbed the keepers of one valuable facility, and prompted William Davies to appeal on their behalf for an allowance of coal to dry their clothes by. It was, he explained, "so far from the Low Light which they are obliged to attend to 4 times each night which occasions their clothes to be very wet".[14]

In 1779 the low light was found to be so decayed that it had to be rebuilt. The following year saw a complete reversal of the erosive tendencies so prevalent in preceding years. The outer sands began to grow to such an extent that the smallest fishing craft had to feel their way cautiously inshore. They did so by keeping the chapel in line with the church. On January 19th, 1782, Trinity House were obliged to issue the following warning:

NOTICE TO MARINERS

This Corporation, having lately caused a survey to be taken of the Stamford, in which was found only three fathoms in the best of the channel at High Water, it is recommended to all Masters and Pilots to be very cautious in navigating ships of a great draught through that Channel.[15]

This trend continued for more than ten years. Gillingwater, writing about 1790, observed that a bank of sand had formed just offshore which remained dry at all states of the tide, and forecast that in years to come this would form the foundations of a new town.[16] It proved to be a false prophecy, for within a few years the entire bank had disappeared.

In 1796 the Trinity Brethren abandoned the reflecting light for which

*See section on Hunstanton.

they had entertained such high hopes and equipped the high light with eleven Argand burners set in the focus of silvered reflectors.

At the same time the two lighthouses were classified as separate stations, each with its own complement of keepers. The high light was put in charge of a keeper named Howard and his wife, who were said to "attend their duty very strictly" and were paid £50 a year for doing so.

For the post of keeper at the low light the Trinity Brethren gave sympathetic consideration to John Harvey, lately mate aboard the Haisbro' lightship, but now cripped with rheumatism and forced ashore. Harvey held this post for the next thirty-six years, until his death at the advanced age of eighty.

With the disappearance of the sandbar Lowestoft Ness was again subjected to severe scouring, and in 1803 the low light once more had to be rebuilt, this time with a larger lantern. In January, 1827, following a severe storm, it was found to be in imminent danger of toppling into the sea and was replaced by a similar structure strengthened by a brick foundation. The new light shone for the first time on the night of 25th February, 1832.

Meanwhile complaints were being made that the high light was underpowered. Oil had brought such improvements to the domestic lighting of the town that the lighthouse was rapidly being eclipsed. The agent, Mr Davies, son of the William Davies who was agent fifty years earlier, went out

Left: The derelict tower of Pakefield lighthouse still standing in the grounds of Pontin's holiday camp.

Opposite: Pakefield cliffs looking towards the site of the lighthouse at the time the light was in operation.

from Yarmouth aboard the lightvessel tender and reported that the lights in some houses were so powerful that it was well-nigh impossible to distinguish the high light. He was instructed to distribute handbills among householders asking them to be sure that their seaward-facing windows were shuttered at night so that the sailors would know for certain which light was the actual lighthouse!

The storms which came with each successive winter not only brought drastic scouring of the coastline but also wrought havoc with the outlying sands which, battered and convulsed by heavy seas, changed their shape beyond all recognition, with a resulting alteration in the course and depth of the channels between. In an attempt to keep pace with these sudden and unpredictable changes Trinity House began, about this time, to introduce subsidiary lights, and mention must be made at this point of three new lighthouses established in the vicinity of Lowestoft within a period of thirty years. In July, 1831, an inspecting party of Elder Brethren recommended that a lighthouse should be built at Pakefield to mark the channel between the Barnard and Newcombe Sands. A site was acquired in the grounds of Pakefield Hall on a low, sandy cliff some 34 feet high. Here was built a circular tower of brickwork surmounted by a lantern containing two Argand oil lamps. The lighthouse was built by Messrs James Taylor of Yarmouth to the design of a London architect, Mr Richard Suter. The cost was £821 9s. 4d. The light

Lowestoft low light, built in 1866, which like its wooden predecessors was designed to be capable of being moved along the beach when changes occurred in the channel. It also had to be moved at times because of erosion.

was displayed for the first time on the night of 1st May, 1832, a fixed red light being visible over a range of nine miles. It was in the care of "old Captain Goodwin, lately retired from the Jamaica trade."[17]

The new lighthouse had a short life however, for by 1850 the channel had shifted so far southward that Pakefield was no longer an effective mark. The light was then moved to the cliffs at Kessingland, some three miles further down the coast, opposite where the course of the channel now lay. This station survived until the early years of the present century. Pakefield was extinguished on 1st December, 1864, at which time a pair of leading lights was set up at Hopton to lead clear of the southern end of the Corton Sand. The high light was built on a slope of rising ground on the seaward side of the former Hopton railway station, and the low light stood on Hopton Denes, a tract of coastal duneland since taken by the sea. These lights were even shorter lived, for by 1871 the Corton Sand had extended so far to the southward that Hopton lights could not be kept in alignment. The tower at Kessingland and the two at Hopton no longer exist, but Pakefield still survives, today forming an integral part of Pontin's Holiday Camp.

Lowestoft high and low lights, seen in a view from the North Battery (the site of Belle Vue Park) in an engraving made by William Daniell in 1822.   *Suffolk County Library, Lowestoft*

To return to Lowestoft, in 1840 a series of complaints was made against the efficiency of the light displayed from the upper lighthouse. Investigations revealed that the keeper, John Bishop, attended the lighthouse each evening only for so long as it took him to light the lamps. He then locked the tower and left it unattended throughout the night while he went off to work as a waiter at a nearby alehouse, for which he was paid five shillings per day and night. There is no indication of the part played by the assistant keeper in this piece of collusion, but he and Bishop were both summarily dismissed. By 1861 the low light was again in a state of bad repair and it was becoming clear that timber was simply not strong enough or sufficiently durable to withstand the ravages of the sea. The Engineer-in-Chief of Trinity House, Mr James Douglass, [18] designed a ncw structure of wrought ironwork capable of being easily moved should circumstances demand it. This came into service in 1867.

In 1870, following experiments with electric lighting at the South Foreland lighthouse and its subsequent adoption at Dungeness in 1862, it was decided that Lowestoft high light should be electrified. The existing tower, which had now stood for close on two hundred years, was not considered strong

Lowestoft high lighthouse a few years before it was replaced by the tower which still stands today.

enough to take the weight of the new equipment. Accordingly, work began in 1872 on building a replacement. The project was carried out by Messrs Suddelay & Stanford, of Beverley in Yorkshire, at a cost of £2,350. It is this tower which still stands today. Owing to the slope of the surrounding ground it proved impossible to house the generating machinery on the same premises. Instead a site was acquired on the opposite side of the Yarmouth Road, beside which the lighthouse stands, and permission was obtained from the local council to run the connecting cables beneath the road surface. Before the tower was ready to receive the new apparatus, however, paraffin oil became available as an illuminant, and it immediately proved itself to be so economical and efficient that it was adopted for use in the new lighthouse in preference to electricity. At the same time a new optical system was fitted having a revolving lens, and the light, which up to then had always been fixed, was made to flash at half-minute intervals. The rebuilding was completed in 1874.

With a flashing character allotted to the upper light, it was not long

106

before a similar change was effected to the low light. The following announcement was published during December, 1880:

NOTICE TO MARINERS

"During the month of January 1881 the Low Light of Lowestoft will be made occulting; that is to say it will, once in every half-minute, suddenly disappear for three seconds and then as suddenly reappear at full power."[19]

No sooner had this alteration taken place than a severe storm caused scouring of the foreshore, necessitating the light being moved some eighty yards back. When first built, the distance between the two lights had been 1,013 yards. In less than fourteen years this had been reduced by a quarter. The lower light had been designed by Mr Douglass so as to be easily moveable, but the keepers' dwellings were not, and these were quickly engulfed by the sea. It was therefore resolved to make the low light an unattended station. At the same time the light-source at both lighthouses was changed to coal gas taken from the town's mains.

The new high lighthouse which came into use in 1874, seen here about 1911. Lowestoft was probably the only Trinity House station with a tram stop outside the door.

By 1894 it was again necessary to move the low light, which was withdrawn to a point 250 yards above high water, though unfortunately this failed to remedy matters for any length of time. The turn of the century saw the completion of defensive works along Lowestoft's entire frontage to the sea, reaching southwards to Pakefield, just in time to save the low light from yet another move, since the tideline had now advanced to within 95 feet of its foundations.

Although these protective measures were highly successful so far as Lowestoft was concerned, they had tragic repercussions elsewhere. One drastic effect of the tidal drift along the East Anglian coast is that wherever the sea encounters any form of obstruction, such as a breakwater, a groyne or a jetty, it will begin to scour the section of coast immediately to the southward with great ferocity. Immediately to the south of Lowestoft's new sea wall stood the village of Pakefield. Almost at once the effects began to manifest themselves as one section of cliff after another subsided. During the succeeding fifty years more than half of Pakefield village, including nearly one hundred inhabited dwellings, was lost to the sea. Not only did the neighbouring section of coast feel the effects, there were equally dramatic results offshore. The most fundamental change to come about was the complete upheaval of the outlying sands and their re-formation further out to sea, which in turn resulted in the total disappearance of the Stanford Channel as it then existed.

By about 1920 the low light had ceased to fulfil any useful function, since the need to maintain Lowestoft lights as a pair ended with the disappearance of the Stanford Channel. The decision was therefore taken to withdraw the low light altogether and to continue the high light as a conventional coastwise beacon. The low light was extinguished for the last time at break of day on 27th August, 1923, and soon afterwards the structure was dismantled and removed. The high light was converted to electricity in July, 1936, nearly seventy years after this form of illumination had first been proposed for it. The new light-source, boosted by twin optical lenses, made this one of the most powerful lights on the entire east coast.

With these innovations complete it was no longer necessary to mount a 24-hour watch, so the lighthouse became a "man and wife" station. This was a posting generally reserved for a senior keeper serving out his time prior to retirement, with his wife officially taken on strength as his assistant. This arrangement remained in force until 1974 when the station was made entirely automatic, with no keeper assigned to it at all.

Such is the role of Lowestoft lighthouse at the present day. From its position on the ridge, nearly 70 feet above the sea, its circular white tower rises to a height of 59 feet, making it 123 feet in all from sea level to the focus of the light. Its lamps and prisms revolve to produce a clear-cut single flash every fifteen seconds, visible over a distance of seventeen miles. From a northward-

The Royal Naval Patrol Service memorial in Belle Vue Park, Lowestoft. Standing close to the lighthouse, it was purposely built to the same height so that the gilded sailing ship on the memorial is lit by the revolving beam of the lighthouse. *D. J. Leech*

facing window, lower in the tower, a fixed subsidiary light, at an elevation of ninety-nine feet, throws a ruby-red beam over the Scroby Sands, three miles off Yarmouth and nine miles distant from the lighthouse.

Historically, Lowestoft has the distinction of being the oldest established lighthouse station on the coasts of Great Britain. From this point, at the easternmost extremity of the British Isles, a light has shone out every night without fail for more than three hundred and seventy years. The only exception to this occurred during the war years when, in common with all lighthouses, the light was displayed only for brief periods, predetermined by the Admiralty, to aid a passing convoy or a flotilla of naval craft.

A park with ornamental gardens now occupies the site where Samuel Pepys's tower once stood, but his plaque still survives. Carefully restored to its authentic heraldic colours, it is preserved inside the tower of the present lighthouse, and is without doubt one of the most historic and treasured possessions of Trinity House.

CHAPTER FIVE

Hunstanton

And to sea, And to sea,
The Float¹ is astern,
South-east they the Light,
Of Hunst'on discern.
(*The Brigantine, Europe*—John R. Simms)

FOR centuries past the Wash has acted as a giant sludgepan, into which the rivers at one end have poured silt and mud scoured from the rich black soil of the Fens, while the sea at the other has deposited sand and shingle carried southward by the powerful tidal currents. In consequence the waters of this large bay have for long been congested by extensive sandbanks and tidal mudflats, so that during periods of extreme low tide as much of the Wash dries out as remains covered by water. By contrast, such navigable channels as do exist contain some of the greatest depths in the southern half of the North Sea. In short, the Wash is an area of quicksands, quagmires and unpredictable tide-races, a statement to which King John would doubtless be willing to testify.

Through this complexity of sand and shallows must pass any ship bound for the ports of Lynn or Boston or the inland port of Wisbech. For nearly the whole of its length the coast forms a low-lying fringe of mud and salt marsh; flat, featureless and devoid of human habitation. Isolated farms and scattered villages are to be found, standing back from the sea on drier and firmer ground. To the marshmen and fen-folk living hereabouts the sea is a remote and inaccessible thing, seen only as a distant streak of silver glinting in the sunlight. In no other part of England is it possible to live on the coast and yet be so far from the sea.

It is Hunstanton, on the sharp bend at the mouth of the Wash, that proves the exception to the rule. Here, a ridge of red and white chalk cliffs rises suddenly from the prevailing flatness to present a mile-long frontage to the sea before subsiding again as abruptly as it began. These cliffs, which run in such clear-cut layers, mark the termination of the chalk seams which branch northwards from the Chilterns and underlie much of the light farming

Hunstanton lighthouse at the turn of the century seen through the ruins of St Edmund's Chapel. The lighthouse was known to seamen as "the Chapel Light."

land of East Anglia. At no other point, however, does the chalk take on the distinctive coloration to be seen at Hunstanton, and it is interesting to note that as far away as the North Riding of Yorkshire chalk is often referred to as Hunstanton Limestone.

According to local legend Edmund, the Saxon king and martyr, landed beneath these cliffs in the year 855 A.D. on his arrival from Germany to claim the kingdom of East Anglia. In commemoration this spot became known as St Edmund's Point, though it is a name that has, regrettably, fallen out of use. About 1272, in keeping with the monastic custom of perpetuating sites of religious importance, there was built on the cliffs overlooking St Edmund's Point a small and isolated chapel, similar to that which Matthew Danthorpe the hermit was to found on the Spurn more than a century later. A few fragments of St Edmund's Chapel still survive to show that it was built of cobblestones and rubblework, augmented here and there by pieces of red chalk taken from the cliff. The site formed part of the lands owned by the le Strange family, the local lords of the manor, who lived in the fine moated hall nearby. The successive heads of this family enjoyed the hereditary title of

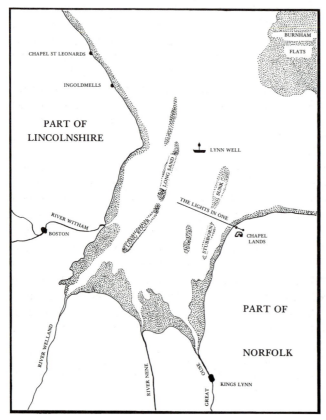

Lord High Admiral of the Wash, and their estates ran down to the sea and out beyond the tideline "as far as a man can ride on horseback and throw a javelin."

To what extent St Edmund's Chapel was ever inhabited is uncertain. One theory suggests that it was the abode of a hermit. Other sources maintain that it housed a small community of monks, thereby acting as a cell to some larger establishment elsewhere. Either way, the fact remains that the site was certainly occupied, with the direct result that the chapel quickly became an established seamark, the lighted windows at night proving faintly discernible to seamen in the darkness, effectively pin-pointing for them the entrance to the Wash. It would hardly have been intended that St Edmund's Chapel should serve the additional purpose of a mark for sailors, and such a role would have come about more by accident than design. The dim glow at the windows came not from candles placed there specially for that purpose but from candles stood before an altar or placed at the foot of some statue. It cannot have been foreseen that men's lives would depend on the few stray beams of light escaping through the seaward-facing windows.

But when this fact was realised, St Edmund's Chapel assumed an even greater significance, combining the role of shrine with that of navigational aid. From then on every care was taken to see that the windows shone as brightly as possible and the lights were tended unceasingly throughout the hours of darkness. The "Chapel Lights" became a familiar and accepted feature of this coast, while on estate maps and sea charts alike, Hunstanton cliffs came to be designated "Chapel Lands".[2] When, after many years, the old chapel itself fell into decay and was superseded by a conventional lighthouse, that lighthouse for the whole of its working life was known to sailors far and wide as "The Chapel Light".

The fifteenth and sixteenth centuries brought added prosperity to the ancient port of Lynn. Its situation, at the point where an intricate network of Fenland rivers found an outfall to the sea, made it the main port of supply and distribution for a vast inland region. In fact no fewer than nine counties relied on their goods being shipped into the port. By the middle of the seventeenth century King's Lynn was second only to London in the quantities of coal it imported, while its shipments of wine were exceeded only by those of London and Bristol. The population of merchants, the nucleus of which had become established during the prosperous era of the woollen trade, rapidly expanded. The narrow streets hard by the waterfront became the sites of large and extravagant mansions, built by the merchants out of their new-found wealth. Daniel Defoe was agreeably impressed:

"Here are more gentry," he declared, "and consequently is more gaiety than in Yarmouth, or even in Norwich itself, the place abounding in very good company."[3]

When this photograph was taken of St Edmund's Chapel at Hunstanton in 1853 sufficient remained for its original proportions to be apparent.

Not least among the hazards facing ships bound for the Wash was the task of negotiating its entrance. Although the Wash is some eighteen miles across its mouth, only a small portion of this width is navigable water. The main channel, running like a backbone down the centre, is hemmed in on either side by submerged sands and shoal waters, over which none but the smallest of craft can safely pass. Ships of burden may sail up and down the Wash, but never across it. The narrowness of the channel demands careful navigation, even by today's standards, but in the days of sail it was a far more exacting and hazardous undertaking. Altogether it would be hard to find a more difficult and deceptive section of coast on which to make a landfall.

As a result of these conditions, more than one prosperous merchant in the port of Lynn or Boston had the misfortune to see his vessel come to grief practically within sight of its own home port. When, in 1663, a syndicate of Lynn merchants put forward a proposal for establishing a lighthouse to indicate the entrance to the Wash, the project met with enthusiastic support from all quarters. For such a lighthouse there could be but one practical location; the commanding height of Hunstanton Cliff, where it would be visible not only across the Wash but for a considerable way along the North Norfolk coast and up the distant coast of Lincolnshire. Furthermore, if the merchants could only procure a patent from the King authorising them to levy tolls on ships trading to the northern coasts, as well as those entering or leaving the Wash, then the whole proposition might turn out most profitably.

A petition was forthwith drawn up, to which many signatures were readily subscribed, headed by that of the Mayor of Lynn, William Wharton. Signatures were also obtained from merchants and mariners in the ports of Boston and Wells, in addition to those of fishermen in the many creeks and harbours in the immediate vicinity. The completed petition, submitted to Charles II on 1st August, 1663, was in the following words:

"WHEREAS the passage upon the coast of Norfolk in and about Lynn channels is much infested with many sands not only very troublesome but exceeding dangerous to all ships passing, that many having perished upon the same sands especially in the night, which might, by God's blessing easily be prevented by erection of lights upon a place called Hunstanton Cliff or Chapel Lands in the said County of Norfolk, to be kept every night in the year, being very necessary for the preservation of our lives, ships and goods. The consideration whereof emboldens us (being fully assured of your Majesty's goodness in furthering so good and necessary a work) humbly to supplicate your Majesty for the granting of Commission for erecting the same lights the charge whereof may be borne by raising of eight pence upon every 20 chalders of coals or twenty tons of other goods and merchandise upon English ships and one penny per ton upon foreign ships trading to and from the port of Lynn and the creeks and members of the same and to and from Boston southwards which we, your Majesty's subjects, are very willing to bear and for which benefit we shall be ever much obliged to pray for your Majesty's long and prosperous reign."[4]

Following set procedure, the petition came before the Privy Council, who in turn referred it to the Brethren of Trinity House for their recommendations. At a meeting of the Trinity House Court held on October 16th a more-or-less favourable reply was drafted:

"MAY IT PLEASE YOUR MOST EXCELLENT MAJESTIE. In obedience to your Majestie's command and reference directed unto the brotherhood of the Trinity House dated the first day of August last past. Upon the humble supplication of Owners and Masters of Shipps and other mariners belonging to the port of King's Lynn in the County of Norfolk with the Creeks and Members of that port and the town of Boston in the County of Lincolnshire for liberty to erect lighthouses upon the Chapel Lands in the County of Norfolk, and having examined and debated the reasons given for the same do find the necessity to be such as is suggested to your Majestie; which being erected will be a probable means for preservation of mens lives and Shipping passing into and from the said ports.

We do therefore upon the whole matter give humble submission that Lighthouses upon the Chapel Lands may be of good use (but only for such Ships as goeth with trade to Lynn and Boston with the Creeks and Members belonging to the said ports) and a work worthy of encouragement."

But at this point the Brethren had some reservations to make. They saw no reason why vessels bound to and from the northern coasts should be obliged to

The house in King's Lynn occupied by John Knight before he fled to the Continent soon after 1650.

contribute to a light which they would be too far out to sea even to catch sight of. The report continued:

"If only that Shipping which derive the benefit will maintain the same and the rest of the Navigation be free from that burthen and derive no benefit thereby, also the inhabitants of the foresaid ports by your Majestie's special command be Constrayned from imposing any charge upon other Shipping and confining them to raise the maintenance for the Lights only from those vessels trading to and from the ports of Lynn and Boston with the Creeks and Members belonging to the same *and not others*."[5]

So the Trinity Brethren were prepared, subject to the foregoing qualifications, to open the door to yet more private enterprise and to suffer a further infringement of their exclusive rights. That they should have allowed this application to go through completely unopposed was in itself most unusual. Perhaps they considered that by making these stipulations they would limit the status of the lighthouse to that of a purely local light, whose earning capacity would not amount to anything worth their while. On the other hand there is a distinct possibility that the Brethren were prompted by more subtle and obscure motives. The Court that drafted the reply was presided over by Sir William Batten, Surveyor-General of the Navy and currently Master of Trinity House. Sir William, even at that moment, was surreptitiously plotting to establish some lights of his own at Harwich. Obviously he could never allow these intentions to become known so long as he held office as Master of Trinity House, since such motives were diametrically opposed to all that the Corporation stood for. But when his term was over he would be free to proceed without attracting too much adverse criticism, and it was therefore vital to Sir William's designs that the Corporation should not raise in the case of Hunstanton objections that might create awkward precedents when the time came for his own proposal to be considered.

It seems quite feasible, then, that Sir William would do his utmost to shepherd the Hunstanton grant through smoothly and without complications. If so he was wasting his time. Unbeknown to Sir William Batten, or to Trinity House, another contender had entered the field; a man whose proven loyalty and undoubted integrity were in themselves sufficient guarantee that the grant would be his, despite the prior claim of the merchants of Lynn and regardless of any objections that Trinity House might make. This other contender was John Knight, personal surgeon to the King.

John Knight and his half-sister, Frances, were children of John Knight the elder by his first and second marriages respectively. The father was for many years Herald Painter to King Charles I, so it was to be expected that the family were brought up staunch royalists. During the Civil Wars the son, who had become a surgeon, was engaged in caring for the sick and wounded among the King's forces. During the Commonwealth period he took up practice in London, but his known royalist sympathies brought such hostility and threats that he was driven to seek safety and seclusion elsewhere. Accompanied by his half-sister, he moved to Lynn, where he fared little better than in London. Eventually John made good his escape to the Continent and joined the royal court in Holland, where he remained in close attendance on the King throughout his exile. In 1660 John Knight was among those on board the *Naseby*, renamed *Royal Charles*, as she carried the newly-proclaimed king back to England. Knight's loyalty and faithful service did not go unrewarded, and following the Restoration he was appointed Serjeant-Surgeon to the King and received a pension of one hundred and fifty pounds a year for life.[6]

Frances Knight, who had remained in Lynn, was now married to Edward Bodham, one of the port's most prosperous and prominent merchants and one of the signatories to the petition seeking establishment of a light on Hunstanton Cliff. As events were to prove, of nearly two hundred subscribers to that document, he alone was destined to derive any material benefit. It must have occurred to Bodham, or was pointed out to him by a shrewd and perceptive wife, that John Knight was not just an illustrious relation but potentially a most powerful and effective ally, and in the present situation concerning the light on Hunstanton Cliff he could be of real service to Bodham. If John Knight could be persuaded to apply for the lighthouse grant in his own name, there was every chance that he would be successful. And when the business had been brought to a favourable conclusion, John Knight could, by way of gift, transfer the patent to his brother-in-law. Edward Bodham would not need to concern himself with supporting a petition which stood little chance of success. He could in the end become the sole beneficiary, and be obliged to share the profits with nobody.

Knight readily agreed to co-operate, but did not make any immediate move. His position ensured that he would know, from the scraps of gossip circulating within the court, if a rival claimant were to come forward. The most serious threat would be if the Trinity Brethren decided to oppose the merchants' petition or put in a counter-claim on their own behalf. But when the Brethren declared themselves in favour of the proposal, and went so far as to commend it as "a work worthy of encouragement," John Knight's position became virtually unassailable.

Exactly a month elapsed between the Trinity Brethren making their report and the petition being granted. At some time during that period John Knight found an opportune moment to put his case to the King. The effect was precisely what might have been expected. Letters Patent were awarded for a term of sixty-one years to John Knight, entitling him to erect a light or lights "to be continually burning in the night season on the ground known as Hunstanton Cliff or Chapel Lands in the County of Norfolk." The rate of tolls was fixed at exactly the figure the merchants had proposed and the restrictions on the liability of vessels to contribute were imposed as suggested by Trinity House. The Letters Patent of Charles II were signed at Westminster on 3rd June, 1665, by which time a pair of lighthouse towers had taken their stand beside the old chapel on Hunstanton Cliff.

It should be borne in mind that Hunstanton, as mentioned in all these proceedings, meant the scattering of dwellings in the vicinity of Hunstanton Hall, and nowadays referred to universally as Old Hunstanton. To the south lay the Chapel Lands, where the ruinous shrine of St Edmund looked out over the Wash. Beyond that stretched an expanse of open grassland, with sheep grazing contentedly on the slopes where one day a brand new seaside community was destined to arise. That community came as a product of the mid-Victorian era, expressly to cater for the new fad of holidaymaking by the sea. It was not, as some guide books would have us believe, a resort with waters of spa-like qualities. It was to be a place essentially for sea-bathing and one of the safest in England into the bargain. Its name was intended to perpetuate local religious ties, but somehow Saint Edmunds failed to roll off the tongue as easily as New Hunstanton. So, by popular consent, New Hunstanton it became, and today the adjective, superfluous and outdated, still lingers. What nobody could foresee was that this new community would rapidly outstrip the old, growing from a village to a fashionable resort, and eventually into a town with urban district status.

But all this was still more than two centuries in the future when John Knight kindled his lights for the first time in October, 1665. From the

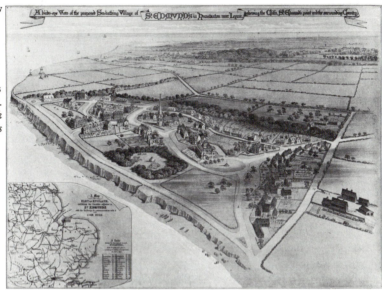

"A birds-eye view of the proposed sea-bathing village of St Edmunds," with the lighthouse and chapel ruins in the upper left.
West Norfolk Photographics

collection of documents now in the safe-keeping of the former King's Lynn Corporation, we know that the lights in their original form consisted of a coal-fired high light and a front light illuminated by candles. There are accounts in respect of building materials including stone, lime and timber delivered to the lighthouse, as well as coal and candles. The precise materials and illuminants, in fact, that might be expected in a station of this type. What is particularly significant is the mention of two additional items, lead and glass, suggesting that the high lighthouse had its fire enclosed within a glazed lantern. Early lights were usually contained in open grates set on top of the tower; only much later did lanterns make their appearance, and when they did they proved a mixed blessing. Enclosing a light automatically cut it off from all natural draught, so that it became necessary for it to be blown with a

Henry Bell's chart of the jurisdiction of the Admiralty of King's Lynn, made in 1693. The chart is orientated with south at the top and needs to be held upside down for the familiar outline of the Wash to become apparent.   *Norfolk Museums Service*

bellows, much in the manner of a blacksmith's forge. It was essential also to have some form of ventilating flue to carry the smoke clear of the lantern. Open braziers, on the other hand, afforded no protection to the fire, or to its keeper, while the problem of preventing the smoke beating down to obscure the light still remained. Furthermore, it is a scientific fact that in coastal districts at night the wind tends to blow from off the land, with the result that an open fire would be fanned to its brightest on the side that was not required to be seen. Nevertheless, the advantages of enclosing a light generally outweighed the disadvantages, so that in time lanterns became a standard feature of lighthouse design.

From two distinct and widely separated sources comes confirmation that the high light at Hunstanton was indeed a closed-in light, coal-fired and bellows-blown. Firstly, John Whormby's account has this to say:

"Hunstanton, — *a close coal light* and a candle or oil light granted to John Knight".[7]

A second reference is to be found in Armstrong's *History of Norfolk*, published about thirty-five years after Whormby's account was written. Describing the new lighthouse with its revolutionary light of oil, which had recently come into service at Hunstanton, the writer makes a significant reference to its predecessor:

"By this construction the light is constant and certain, whereas the seamen were sometimes obliged to awaken the old gentleman at the former lighthouse with a shot, to put him in mind that his fire wanted blowing."

Besides being amusing, that description is highly informative, since the fact that the fire needed blowing at all indicates that it must have been closed in.

The two cases generally accepted as the earliest examples of enclosed fire lights are Lowestoft, where the Trinity Brethren glazed their existing coal light in 1677, and St Agnes, built in 1680 with a lantern inherent in its design. Hunstanton emerges as an even earlier example, having been in commission some twelve years before the conversion at Lowestoft took place.

On 20th February, 1666, four months after the lighthouses came into service, John Knight put his name to a document assigning his rights and interests in the patent to the joint ownership of Edward and Frances Bodham. Under the laws then governing man and wife property, this in effect made Edward Bodham the new legal owner. With this transaction completed John Knight's contribution in the matter was at an end. He had stepped only briefly on stage to play out the leading role, but as a result of his intervention Edward Bodham was, to all intents and purposes, sole proprietor of the Chapel Lights, a position he would never have attained had it not been for John Knight.

It might be surmised that the somewhat devious means by which Edward Bodham came into possession of the lighthouses would have given rise to a certain resentment among his associates who had put their names to the original petition, but if it did the feeling was short lived. Edward Bodham became an increasingly prosperous and popular figure in the port. Among his many activities was that of local correspondent for the *London Gazette*, supplying weather information and particulars of shipping arrivals and departures. He was elected Mayor of Lynn for the year 1685-86, and died in 1688 at the age of 58. His widow survived for a further twelve years to enjoy the sole benefit of the lights. She died in 1700 and under the terms of her will made the previous year her son Edward inherited the patent.

Edward Bodham the younger, Captain Edward, as he was sometimes styled, had been born in 1662 and had spent much of his 38 years travelling abroad, finally settling in Norway with his Norwegian wife, Gardrut. In no position to assume the personal responsibility of maintaining lights in the night season on Hunstanton Cliff, Edward appointed his brother-in-law, Robert Awborne, to act as agent on his behalf. Edward survived his mother by only four years, dying in Norway on 1st November 1704, and his body was brought home and interred in St Margaret's church, King's Lynn, where a memorial tablet can be seen in the Lady Chapel. In accordance with her husband's will, Gardrut Bodham inherited the ownership of the Chapel Lights, the revenue from which was made payable to her in Norway.

The lease had now run for more than half its allotted term, and sooner or later the problem of obtaining a renewal would have to be faced. So it was that in 1710 proceedings commenced to secure the patent for a further term, to take effect when the current lease expired in 1726. Being neither of British nationality nor resident in this country, Gardrut Bodham was by no means the ideal person to make such an application. Instead it was arranged for the petition to be submitted in the joint names of Rebecca Everard, eldest of the late Edward Bodham's three sisters, and her husband, James Everard. What mattered most was the fact that she was a niece of John Knight.

James Everard is described in Hillen's *History of the Borough of King's Lynn* as a wealthy banker, but this statement is discredited in Calvert's *History of Hunstanton Lighthouse*, published in 1939. This exhaustive genealogical study of those connected with the lighthouse provides evidence to show that Hillen was confusing Everard with later generations of the same name, and that the banking partnership of Everard and Blencowe did not come into being until 1826.[8] Instead, the author identifies James Everard as the Vicar of Middleton, a village about four miles from King's Lynn.

The reason for this joint application was two-fold. Firstly, it was hoped that James Everard's standing as a man of the Church, coupled with his wife's direct relationship to the original patentee, would qualify them in preference to any other contender who might appear. Secondly, ever since the death of Frances Bodham in 1700, James and Rebecca Everard had been passed off as the legal owners, a piece of collusion which had been perpetrated in order to conceal the fact that the patent had passed into the hands of an owner who was living in a foreign land. Edward Bodham had, in fact, signed a deed transferring his interest to his sister Rebecca and her husband, though this was nothing more than a paper transaction. The net profits had continued to be surrendered to Edward Bodham in Norway up to the time of his death in 1704, and since then they had been paid to the widow, Gardrut Bodham, and would continue so during her lifetime. Only in the event of her death would James and Rebecca Everard become owners of the patent in anything but mere name. It was vital that the name of Edward Bodham should not figure in any affairs connected with the lighthouse and that the existence of his Norwegian wife should be kept a close secret.

The petition was put before the Lords of the Treasury in January, 1710. [9] With it were sent certain documents supporting the petitioners' claim to the patent, including the original grant to John Knight, the deed whereby he signed over his interest to Edward and Frances Bodham, the will of Edward Bodham, Senior, and the deed by which the younger Edward Bodham ostensibly relinquished ownership in favour of James and Rebecca Everard. Particulars of receipts and disbursements accompanied these papers, but there was nothing to reveal what had become of the difference between the two totals. The only reference to Norway was in a note explaining that one of the documents was not the original but a copy thereof; "the original was carried by Mr Edward Bodham, the son, into Norway where he died without issue, and the same not since to be found."

In due course the application reached Trinity House in London, where it came before a Court of Elder Brethren in September, 1710. After much debate, a report was sent to the Lords of the Treasury stating that the Corporation was opposed to the application.[10] If only the Brethren had known that there existed books of account showing that for some years the profits had been surrendered to a resident in a foreign land, and had they taken the opportunity to read Edward Bodham's will, in which those profits were bequeathed to a Norwegian wife, of whom they were in complete ignorance, the outcome would doubtless have been different. As it was, the Corporation could only base its objections on the grounds of its ancient and exclusive rights to erect and maintain seamarks. This by itself proved insufficient, and the Brethren's case was overruled by the Crown. In February, 1711, more than a year after the petition had been submitted, Letters Patent were issued to James Everard, Clerk, and Rebecca his wife, renewing the patent in their favour for a 'further fifty years.[11] With the lease now secure until 1761, the practice of remitting the revenue to Gardrut Bodham could be resumed. She was still in receipt of this income when she died in 1723, and from then on the benefit passed solely to Rebecca Everard, since her husband had died the previous year.

So far as can be judged, the remaining thirty-eight years of this term were punctuated by only one event of importance, the discontinuation of the front light some time between 1738 and 1750. There is nothing in the records to show precisely when this happened. Candles were still being purchased in quantity up to 1738, while Whormby's account in 1746 specifically mentions a coal light and "a candle or oil light." (It is surprising that the normally thorough and painstaking John Whormby did not make quite certain which.) That is the last time that any reference is to be found either to a front light or to candles. Coal continued to be the main item of expenditure right up to the time that the fire light was dispensed with in 1778, and only then does oil begin to feature in the accounts.

In 1751, ten years in advance of the current term expiring, Rebecca Everard petitioned for a further extension. This application does not appear to have encounted so much opposition as the previous one, and despite the fact that Trinity House recommended against it Mrs Everard received a grant from George II securing the patent in her favour for fifty years, terminating in 1801.[12] She died in 1755, bequeathing the grant to her eldest son, Edward. A prominent citizen and alderman of King's Lynn, Edward Everard lived in the house in Nelson Street formerly occupied by John Knight. He had already served that town as its Mayor during the year 1742 and was destined to do so again in the near future. At the time he inherited the lighthouse, he was fifty-six years old, with a wife, Mary, by whom he had a son, born in 1739, who also took the name of Edward.

When the elder Edward Everard died in 1769 the remaining thirty-two years of the term devolved to his son, Edward, variously described as a merchant, a shipowner, a wine importer and a general chandler. He was all of these, but only to a degree. Above all he was a brewer of beer, being the owner of a sizeable brewery in Baker Lane. To these varied activities was added, on 27th February, 1769, that of lighthouse proprietor. He was, in fact the seventh individual owner to reap the benefit of the lights on Hunstanton Cliff, and circumstances would shortly compel him to be the first of them to introduce any significant improvement.

The patent had now been in existence for just over one hundred years and during that time the only radical change to have taken place was the disappearance of the front light. This had come about by the culmination of physical changes in the coastline, changes which had evolved slowly and gradually. There was nothing of that nature about the next change, which came suddenly and unexpectedly, in the form of a devastating fire, towards the end of 1777. No details have survived to show exactly what happened, but

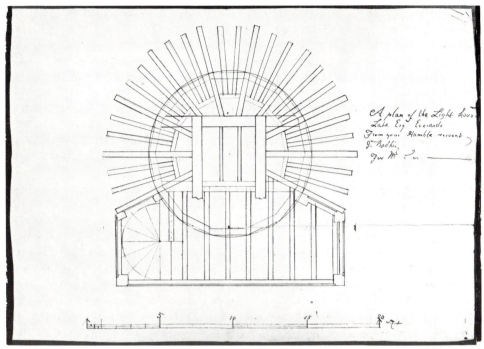

A scale plan of the tower built at Hunstanton in 1776 by Edward Everard.

it is reasonable to suppose that a stray spark or falling cinder started a fire that could not be controlled and resulted in the total destruction of the whole premises. No attempt to repair the damage was made, or even contemplated; it was necessarily a case of rebuilding the station.

The tower that took its stand upon Hunstanton Cliff was a plain and simple structure, the working drawings of which still exist. These show a circular tower, 33 feet in height, with a base 11 feet in diameter, tapering to 8 feet at the top. The lantern surmounting it bore more resemblance to a look-out than a lantern, being nothing more than a square box with a sloping roof and glazing on the seaward side only. Construction was of timber throughout, which, considering the fate of the previous tower, seems to have been tempting Providence. But if Mr Everard's new tower had little to recommend it, this was certainly not the case with the lighting equipment that it housed. In finding someone to undertake this side of the project, Edward Everard did not have to look far. In his own home town of Lynn lived a man by the name of Ezekiel Walker, a philosopher, a physicist and a prolific writer of scientific tracts. Many of Mr Walker's essays had been published in Nicholson's

125

Philosophical Journal, covering a diversity of subjects, such as "An Aparatus for the Conducting of Sound and Holding Conversations at a Distance", "A Standard of Light for Comparing all Other Lights" and a description of a device for snuffing candles without causing smoke. Of more than twenty such papers, the majority were concerned in one way or another with optics or illumination. Ezekiel Walker seemed ideally suited to the task of lighting Mr Everard's new lighthouse, and he began by carrying out a study of the developments in illumination that had recently taken place in the vicinity of Liverpool, where two lighthouses on the Mersey, one at Hoylake and the other at Bidston, had been fitted with large reflectors made of wood, hollowed out and lined with facets of silvered glass.

By carrying this experiment a stage further, Ezekiel Walker devised an apparatus for Hunstanton which revolutionised lighthouse illumination. Instead of a single reflector, Mr Walker installed a number of smaller ones made of sheet copper plated with pure silver and polished to a mirror finish. Copper coated with silver is what the jewellery trade knows as Sheffield Plate, and it was the Sheffield Plate Company who produced eighteen such reflectors for Mr Walker in their workshops at Long Acre, London. However, the key to success lay not so much in the size or number of reflectors as in their shape. Here Ezekiel Walker applied his scientific knowledge to good effect. By fashioning each reflector to a true parabolic curve, he was able to set an oil lamp precisely in the focal centre, at the point where the light rays would be concentrated to their maximum intensity. The new lighthouse was lit for the first time one night in 1778 and shone out with a brilliance that made all others of its kind appear dim by comparison. For the first time, a major coast light was in commission making use of an illuminant other than coal. Ezekiel Walker, though he could not claim the actual invention, had nevertheless succeeded in perfecting catoptric lighting, soon to become the standard at all lighthouses.

To the credit of Edward Everard it could be said that he had lost no time, and spared no expense, in providing a replacement for the Chapel Light; a replacement that was as efficient and up-to-date as the skill of the day could make it. This example would speak well for him when the time came to apply for a renewal of the lease. That time was not long in coming. In 1781, with the outstanding term reduced to exactly twenty years, Edward Everard petitioned for a further term when the present lease had run its course. The petition began by emphasising the great benefit that navigation derived from the lighthouse and went on to relate that recently a disastrous fire had consumed the former tower and that the petitioner had, at his own proper cost and charges, built a new one in its stead. The application was supported by a sworn declaration that the cost of building the replacement amounted to £850[13] and that the average income per year was £264, against which the average disbursements totalled £117 per year. In view of the narrow margin of profit, Mr Everard prayed that he might be granted a renewal of the lease to enable him to recoup the expense to which he had been put. There were forty-three signatures supporting the application, including that of the Mayor of Lynn, Robert Freeman, but the proposal encountered strong opposition from the Brethren of Trinity House. It was six years before a decision was reached, but when it finally came the verdict went in favour of Edward Everard, who was granted a further lease of thirty-six years to commence on 16th October, 1801, when the current term was due to expire.

The following description of the lighthouse was written about the year 1802:

"To the west of Brancaster and the said great Malthouse, and not far off, is the village of Hunstanton, or Hunston as it is most commonly called, near to which, on a cliff overlooking Lynn Roads and the entrance to Lynn Haven, and elevated 90 feet above high water mark stands the Hunston Lighthouse, which is upon a different construction from other English lighthouses and supposed superior to any of them. It is lighted by Lamps and reflectors instead of coals on a much improved and very judicious plan, the merit of which is due to Mr Walker of Lynn by whom it was invented and under whose direction it was here erected in 1778. This light is communicated by 18 concave reflectors each of 18 inches diameter. They are fixed upon two shelves, one placed over the other in such a manner that the strongest light may be seen where it is most wanted. In the N. × E. direction a strong light is necessary for ships to avoid the dangerous sands and shoals on the Lincolnshire coast. Here, therefore, are placed 7 reflectors in the space of two points of the compass which will appear at some distance as one light. In other directions a weaker light is sufficient. A single reflector with a lamp of 10 single threads of cotton placed in the focus of the curve, which is a parabola, will appear at 15 miles distance larger than a star of the first magnitude, that is, if the glass be kept clean and the lamp trimmed, otherwise instead of light there will no doubt be obscurity for which no blame can attach to the projector. Ten single threads of cotton to each of those 18 lamps make in all 180. Now a street lamp in London is said to contain 28 single threads, and if we divide 180 by 28 we shall have six and one seventh, hence the oil consumed in the Hunston Lighthouse is less than that consumed by 7 London street lamps."[14]

Some extravagant claims have been made on behalf of this light; among them the assertion that it was visible for twenty-one miles out to sea. For nine years it stood unique on the coasts of Britain, and when Mr Walker's invention was ultimately adopted elsewhere it was not Trinity House but the

Commissioners for Northern Lighthouses who took up his idea. Not that the Trinity Brethren were oblivious to the need for improved lighting; the fact was, that they were already experimenting with an alternative design of their own.[15]

The figures quoted by Edward Everard in his petition showed that there was about £150 per annum nett profit from the lighthouse. If this amount stayed the same, it would be about six years before the cost of building could be recouped. On the other hand, a new and advanced lighthouse such as this, with its lease secure for many years to come, would command an attractive price on the open market. Possibly with these considerations in mind Edward Everard, within a few months of renewing his grant, decided to offer the

Hunstanton lighthouse seen in a photograph taken soon after the new prismatic lens was installed in 1863. *Norfolk County Library*

property, lock, stock and barrel to Trinity House. The Trinity Brethren declared that the Chapel Light served only local needs and that they were not interested in acquiring it. But Mr Everard had no difficulty in finding somebody who was, the Collector of Customs for the Port of Lynn, Mr Samuel Lane. If anyone possessed a true knowledge of the earning capacity of the Chapel Light it was surely Samuel Lane, who like his counterparts elsewhere combined his duty as Collector of Customs with that of Collector of Light Dues. Samuel Lane took possession of Hunstanton Lighthouse early in 1788.

By 1807 it was obvious that the lighthouse, once years ahead of its time, was fast becoming outdated. Great strides in the science of illumination and light projection had been made during the thirty years since Ezekiel Walker had installed his revolutionary apparatus, the most significant undoubtedly being the invention in 1784 of a new patent oil lamp. This had proved the most powerful, safe and economical burner yet devised, and it prompted the Trinity Brethren to abandon the reflecting lights for which they had entertained such high hopes at Lowestoft and elsewhere in favour of Argand patent lamps at all English stations. The acknowledged expert in this field was Mr George Robinson, consultant engineer to Trinity House, and in October, 1807, following a series of complaints against the light, Samuel Lane sought his advice. Mr Robinson recommended the installation of a cluster of Argand lamps set in silver-plated reflectors, and also advocated the building of a new tower of brick to alleviate the risk of fire, ever present in the existing timber structure.

For all the difference that it made, Mr Robinson might well have saved himself the trouble. The lighthouse remained unaltered, despite the continued complaints of shipmasters navigating the Wash. When in 1822 the Select Committee published their recommendation that no existing private leases should be renewed at the end of their terms in being the Trinity Brethren at last came to realise that, local light or not, they would sooner or later be obliged to assume ownership of Hunstanton lighthouse, and this being the case, it might as well be sooner. On 5th November, 1825, Jacob Herbert, Secretary of Trinity House, addressed a letter to Samuel Lane, offering to purchase the lighthouse from him. Samuel Lane sent his reply on 9th November, 1825:

> "It is not my present intention to dispose of the Hunstanton Lighthouse, but should I or my Trustee hereafter see cause to part with it you may depend that the first offer shall be made to the Corporation of the Trinity House, well knowing their liberality towards promoting the public good and for whom I entertain great respect, having received repeated favours from them during the time I was so long employed as collector for their Light Duties at Lynn."[16]

In February, 1826, Parliament issued an Order in respect of all privately-owned lighthouses, requiring the following returns to be made:

1. AN ACCOUNT of all Lighthouses in the hands of private Individuals held by Grant or Lease from the Corporation of Trinity House.
2. AN ACCOUNT of all Lighthouses in the hands of private Individuals held by Grant or Lease from the Crown.

There were four lighthouses owned by Trinity House which they had leased to private proprietors, the Smalls, Mumbles, Longships, and Burnham lighthouses in Somerset. Five stations were left in private hands. These were Hunstanton, Winterton and Orford Ness (these two being held jointly), Harwich and Dungeness.[17]

The Order, clearly a preliminary step towards granting statutory powers to Trinity House to take over the remaining private concessions, caused Samuel Lane to have second thoughts about disposing of his interests to the Corporation. He promptly sent a letter to Trinity House informing them that he would now be interested in selling the property. The figure he asked was based on an assessment of the nett profits over the preceding fourteen years;

"Hence," he concluded, "I have a well founded belief on a moderate computation of the value of the whole entireity of this estate by men of knowledge and liberality, that it cannot be worth less than £6,380 and that sum I shall be willing to accept for the same, should the Corporation think it proper to become the purchasors."

At such a figure, the Corporation thought it far from proper, and there the matter rested for the next ten years.

In 1828 there came a significant improvement to the lighting of the Wash. On 21st February that year Trinity House stationed a lightvessel at the head of the Long Sand in the mouth of the Wash and gave it the name "Lynn Well."[18] By 1832 the reliability of Hunstanton lighthouse had become a matter of such concern that a petition was raised bearing thirty-two signatures and submitted to Samuel Lane:

"We, the undersigned Ship-Masters belonging to the Port of Lynn, beg to state our opinion of the inefficiency of the Light at Hunstanton and our anxious desire that some improvement should be taken for the better security of the vessels and the lives of those persons navigating the Deeps."

This at last had some effect, and improvements were forthwith put in hand, including the new set of reflectors which George Robinson had advocated twenty-seven years before. This action may have been prompted by the fact that at the time of the above petition Samuel Lane had successfully applied for an extension of the lease to commence on October 16th, 1837. Mr Lane would

Hunstanton cliffs and lighthouse about 1905, by which time the tower had been painted with red bands.

naturally be anxious at such a time that no criticism of the light should come to offical notice. It is most strange that he should have managed to secure an extension at all, in view of the recommendations made by the Select Committee on Foreign Trade ten years previously.

Samuel Lane died the following year at the age of eighty-six, and the lighthouse now became the property of his son Frederick. He, at least, showed willing from the start. His first action on acquiring the lighthouse was to seek permission from Trinity House for those reflectors which bore upon the Roaring Middle Sand to be coloured red. Alas for Frederick Lane's initial burst of enthusiasm, his tenure of the Chapel Light was destined to be very brief. The next year, on 13th August, 1836, there came before Parliament the Act empowering Trinity House to take over the remaining privately-owned lighthouses, together with their outstanding leases. Vesting Day was fixed for 1st January, 1837.

It was decided to assess each owner's interest in accordance with the earnings of their respective lighthouses during the three preceding years. Hunstanton was not, as we have seen, a tremendous money earner when compared with some lighthouses on the coast. During the three-year period from 1823 to 1825 inclusive, when the lights at Winterton and Orford Ness earned between them a nett profit of £13,414,[19] the Chapel Light yielded only £1,367. Consequently the figure that Frederick Lane could expect to receive in compensation would be far less than that which was offered to some other owners, although it would be arrived at by exactly the same formula. Mr Lane

refused to accept such a differentiation and tried all he knew to command a higher price, and at Vesting Day Hunstanton remained the only lighthouse for which a purchase price had not been agreed, with the matter awaiting the verdict of a tribunal. Mr Lane did, however, sign an agreement giving Trinity House the right to claim the tolls as from 1st January, 1837, pending the hearing of his appeal. The case was finally settled on 9th March that year, the sum awarded to Frederick Lane in respect of the unexpired portion of the current lease and compensation for the extended term which would have begun on 16th October, 1837, amounting to £1,605. This figure was only concerned with Mr Lane's interest in the two leases, and did not include the value of the lighthouse itself or the site on which it stood. With these additional considerations taken into account, the total cost to Trinity House of acquiring the Chapel Light was £2,696.[20]

With the formalities of the purchase completed, the Trinity Brethren made immediate plans to replace the timber structure, which had now been standing for sixty years. In its place was built the tower which survives today. It was commenced in 1838, and consisted of a stone plinth supporting a circular tower of brickwork, 63 feet from base to gallery. On this was placed a lantern

Opposite:
Hunstanton
lighthouse in the
early years of this
century with the
wireless
telegraphy
station on the
left. Note the
vertical strip of
ruby glass in the
lantern.

Right: The
lighthouse as it
stood, disused
and decapitated,
during the
inter-war years.

12 feet in diameter, containing Argand lamps and polished reflectors, producing a concentrated light at an elevation of 109 feet above sea level. The building work was carried out by Messrs William Candler, of King's Lynn, and the lighting equipment was installed by the Newcastle firm of Joseph Cookson. Samuel Lane's idea of red reflectors facing the Roaring Middle was maintained, but over the remaining arc of its coverage the lighthouse showed a fixed white light. It shone for the first time on the night of 3rd September, 1840.

In 1863 the lighting equipment was removed and replaced by a triple-wick oil lamp and a lens consisting of 128 glass prisms which had the effect of magnifying the light to an intensity of 12,750 candle-power. The red sector was achieved by inserting a narrow strip of ruby glass in the lantern glazing, thereby producing a red beam, one mile wide, at the Roaring Middle. Some contemporary guide books on Hunstanton describe its lighthouse as casting a red beam across the Wash. This, of course, only applied in the direction of the Roaring Middle. From other points of the compass it was seen as an ordinary white light.

Lighthouses are designed above all to be functional, and should not be judged by any aesthetic standards. Nevertheless it was widely held that Hunstanton lighthouse, at the peak of its career, ranked as one of the most attractive and pleasingly-proportioned lighthouse stations on our coasts.

In 1872 the merchants and shipowners of King's Lynn were successful in applying to Trinity House for an additional floating light to be established off the Lincolnshire coast at the Inner Dowsing Shoal.[21] Six years later, the lighting of the Wash was further augmented when King's Lynn Corporation positioned a lightvessel at the Bar Flat, where the Lynn, Wisbech and Boston channels enter Lynn Deeps. In 1907, this vessel was moved to a new location north-east of the Roaring Middle, and from then on was known by that name.

Vessels coming from the north now had the benefit of six floating lights to assist them in their passage into the Wash. These were the Humber, off the mouth of that river, the Inner Dowsing and her companion vessel, the Outer Dowsing, in addition to the Dudgeon, Lynn Well and Roaring Middle lightvessels. This chain of floating lights rendered the presence of a light on shore at Hunstanton superfluous, but the outbreak of the First World War delayed any move to close the station down. Hunstanton now took on the

Left: The Lynn Well lightship at Norwich in 1977 after being sold out of service.

Opposite: The former Hunstanton lighthouse as it appears today through the scant remains of St Edmund's Chapel.

134

additional role of an Admiralty wireless station, with local gossip insisting that it was intercepting German messages and breaking their codes.

Early in 1921 Trinity House announced the intention of discontinuing the light, which was lit for the last time on the night of 29th September, 1921. The following evening St Edmunds Point was in darkness for the first time in more than 256 years. On Thursday, 5th January, 1922, at Hunstanton Town Hall, the entire premises, with the exception of the lantern and optical equipment, were sold by auction for £1,300. Between the two wars the decapitated tower stood unused, while the ancillary premises became tearooms.

On the outbreak of the Second World War the former lighthouse was commandeered by the military authorities for use as an observation post, resulting in it gaining a brickwork extension above the gallery, identical to that of its counterpart at Winterton. When peace returned it was acquired by the then Hunstanton Urban District Council who leased it out, firstly to a commercial enterprise and later as living accommodation. It was eventually sold by them in 1965 to a private purchaser who converted the entire property to a delightful seaside residence.

CHAPTER SIX

Harwich

"To Sir W. Batten's, who is going out of town to
Harwich tomorrow to set up a light-house
there which he hath lately got a patent from the
King to set up, that will turn much to his
profit."

(Pepys—Diary 3.1.1665)

SAMUEL Pepys confines this entry to a plain statement of fact, adding little
by way of comment or criticism. Yet from the opinions and convictions
which he expresses elsewhere, there can be little doubt that it was a move
which he deplored wholeheartedly. What must have seemed particularly
disconcerting to him was the fact that this latest bid to establish a lighthouse
was being made by a man who was not only a friend and colleague but an
Elder Brother of Trinity House, who had only recently completed a term as
Master. It was not without good reason that Pepys remarked "Even the Trinity
House has grown corrupt and useless."[1]

Sir William Batten was an elderly, stockily-built seadog of almost rotund
appearance, many years older than Pepys, with a lifetime of naval service
behind him.[2] His name first comes to notice in September, 1638, when, as
Captain William Batten, he "kissed the King's hand for the Surveyor's place."
Apparently there had been "much striving" for this position but "the King
with the help of somebody else thought him the fittest man."[3] One wonders
who that somebody was, and the precise nature of their "help". Batten
retained the surveyorship until 1642, when he returned to sea in command of
the *Greyhound*. England was now in a state of civil war, with the fleet actively
supporting Parliament. Despite a number of notable exploits at sea Batten was
not a dyed-in-the-wool republican and in 1647, accused of lack of zeal, was
relieved of his command. His reaction was to turn a fleet of naval vessels over
to Charles II in Holland. For this he was knighted, but he then withdrew from
active service and was not heard of again throughout the whole of the
Commonwealth period.

At the Restoration in 1660 Sir William was promptly reappointed to his
former post of Surveyor-General. As such he took his place among the other

Harwich high lighthouse, built by General
Francis Slater Rebow in 1817, seen in a print
published by George Virtue in 1834.

137

principal officers of the Navy Board which now included Samuel Pepys, newly appointed to the post of Clerk of the Acts. From this time on the name of Sir William Batten occurs repeatedly in the pages of Pepys' diary, in which Sir William is revealed as a thoroughly unscrupulous individual for whom Pepys had little real liking. It could be argued that if Samuel Pepys genuinely disliked and mistrusted Sir William as intensely as the entries in his diary suggest, why then did he seek to spend so much of his leisure-time in Sir William's company? When considering this point due account must be taken of Pepys' position. As Clerk of the Acts he occupied a post generally considered to be less important than the other three principal officers, and unlike them he could boast neither rank nor experience in the service which they helped to administer. Consequently it behoved Samuel to keep on the right side of Sir William both socially and professionally. They became, on the surface, the best of friends, occupying adjoining houses in Seething Lane and frequently borrowing money from each other, while their respective wives squabbled almost incessantly.

It should be realised also that Sir William, when bent on pleasure, proved himself to be lively and enjoyable company and Pepys makes no secret of the

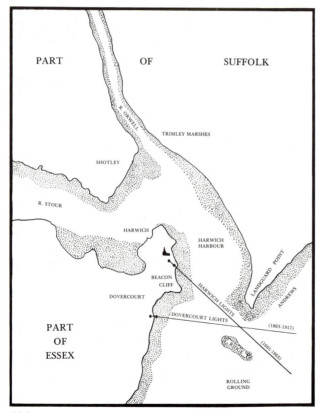

fact that he found the evenings of music and conviviality spent with Sir William at the *Dolphin Inn,* a hostelry in Seething Lane, London, near to where Pepys lived, much to his liking. But to associate freely with Sir William Batten, the rumbustious, hard-living, drinking companion of an evening was one thing. To work through the day, subservient to Sir William Batten, the shifty and dilatory administrator, who lined his pockets at the navy's expense; who turned a blind eye to the blatant sharp practice going on around him; and who connived to misappropriate the sailors' benefit fund known as the Chatham Chest; this was a different proposition altogether. Only in the pages of his diary could Pepys reveal his true feelings. "A lazy, corrupt and doating rogue" was his assessment of Sir William on one occasion,[4] while on another he remarks despairingly "I perceive that the corruptions of the Navy are of so many kinds that it is endless to look after them, especially when such a one as Sir William Batten discourages every man that is honest."[5]

Harwich stands at the northern extremity of the Essex coast, with the combined outflow of the rivers Stour and Orwell separating it from the neighbouring county of Suffolk. The confluence of these two rivers creates a wide expanse of water immediately to the rear of Harwich, enclosed to the north by the land-mass of Suffolk. The result is a natural harbour, sheltered enough to be calm under the stormiest conditions, deep enough to be serviceable at all states of the tide, and sufficiently spacious to accommodate vessels in considerable numbers.

> "I have known," says Daniel Defoe, "that there has been 100 sail of men of war and their attendants, and between three and four hundred sail of collier ships all in this harbour at a time, and yet none of them crowding or riding in danger of one another."[6]

Never were these advantages more readily appreciated, or more fully exploited, than during the Dutch Wars of the seventeenth century. Since in each of these the fundamental point at issue concerned the domination of the seas, they were essentially naval conflicts, and Harwich, with its excellent facilities and its proximity to the enemy coast, found itself the main operational base for the English fleet. The first war in this series of three, between 1652 and 1654, proved inconclusive, and the period that followed was one of uneasy peace. In 1664 the situation again flared up and it became clear that open hostilities could not be avoided for much longer. Consequently Harwich again became the centre of feverish activity as the fleet was hastily re-commissioned.

These vital and urgent preparations brought Sir William Batten post haste to Harwich in the early summer of 1664. As Surveyor-General his was the responsibility of seeing the fleet armed and victualled and made ready for sea. Almost immediately Batten began to explore the possibilities of establishing a lighthouse here. It seems likely that he had already resolved to acquire a grant for himself if ever the opportunity came his way, possibly without having any particular location in mind, and what he saw and heard of the port of Harwich convinced him that that was a likely place.

Sir William questioned local shipmasters and merchants, learning all he could of the dangers offshore and the means taken to avoid them. Vessels approaching from the south, he was told, watched out for a sight of Orford Castle, further up the coast, and by keeping it well clear of Bawdsey Cliffs succeeded in avoiding the Ridge, a shallow sand in the middle of the open stretch of water known as the Rolling Ground. Ships from the north lined up the spire of Harwich church with the Great Brewhouse which stood on Landguard Point, thereby hopefully clearing the Cork Sand. But the main hazard lay nearer to the harbour mouth. Tucked away under the lee of Landguard Point, the Andrews Shoal reached half-way across the channel into the harbour. In order to enter Harwich, a vessel had to pick its way gingerly between this shoal and the Ridge. Sir William must have been greatly encouraged by all that he was told. If ever a place was tailor-made for a pair of leading lights, this was certainly it.

Before many months had passed he was busy collecting signatures to a petition calling for leading lights to mark the passage into Harwich. There was no lack of support. Doubtless the local mariners and merchants welcomed the news that a move was afoot to establish lights at the harbour entrance, with no less a person than the Surveyor-General of the King's Navy and lately Master of Trinity House personally raising the petition. They were not to know that if a

The skyline of Harwich, dominated by the spire of St Nicholas's Church and the high light built by General Rebow.

means was to be provided of lighting the way to Harwich, Sir William Batten did not have it in mind that Trinity House should have any say in the matter.

The completed petition, which bore the signatures of twenty-seven of the leading shipmasters of Harwich, was submitted to the Privy Council on 27th September, 1664. It was immediately referred to the Corporation of Trinity House for their observations. A Court of Elder Brethren considered it on 2nd November, under the Presidency of Sir George Carteret, another character brought to life in the pages of Pepys' diary, who had succeeded Sir William Batten as Master during the previous May. After due debate a reply was addressed to James, Duke of York, in his capacity as President of the Council:

"MAY IT PLEASE YOUR ROYAL HIGHNESS: In obedience to your Highnesses commands in pursuance of the reference dated 21st of October last directed unto the Brethren of the Trinity House upon the petition of Sir William Batten, Knight, Surveyor of his Majesties Navey who humbly proposed the erecting of Lighthouses at Harwich in the county of Essex.

That Lights in the said place will in all respects prove as useful and necessary (for the Navigation trading that way) as any Lights in his Majesties dominions and is a work worthy of encouragement."[7]

It was Hunstanton all over again. For the second time in less than eighteen months the Trinity Brethren sat back and permitted a lighthouse grant to fall straight into the hands of an unscrupulous private speculator. More surprisingly still, they appeared quite unperturbed by the fact that the speculator in this case was a senior member and lately Master of their own fraternity. Clearly the Brethren did not view this proposal as a serious threat to their monopoly.

It would be asking rather much to surmise that Sir William had succeeded in corrupting an entire board of Elder Brethren, so there must have been other valid reasons for this lack of opposition. Two distinct possibilities suggest themselves, either or both of which would account for such a casual attitude. Firstly, from previous instances it becomes evident that Trinity House tended to be jealous of its monopoly only when a major project threatened it. Applications to erect lighthouses on prominent headlands for the benefit of, and supported by the entire coasting trade, were resisted by the Corporation with every means at its disposal. On the other hand the Brethren appeared less perturbed by attempts to establish lights of purely local benefit, and whilst they seldom went to the lengths of recommending or encouraging such projects, their resistance was invariably less intense.

Hunstanton may be regarded as an exceptional case. It could well have rated as a major coastwise light (and ultimately did so) but the Corporation was careful to reduce it to the status of a local beacon serving only the area of the Wash before giving their blessing to John Knight's proposal. Almost certainly the Trinity Brethren took it for granted that Harwich would be similarly restricted; not by any conditions that they themselves might seek to impose, but by the configuration of the coastline. The Naze protruding on one side and Landguard Point on the other made Harwich anything but a salient point, and only shipping directly approaching the harbour would derive any real benefit from its lights, or be liable to contribute tolls to their upkeep.

Secondly, there was the question of precedent. The Trinity Brethren could hardly hope to sustain objections in the case of Harwich when only recently they had actively encouraged a similar project at Hunstanton. This might well have been what Sir William Batten was counting on when, during his term as Master, the Hunstanton grant was hustled through virtually unopposed.

Whatever the reasons for this lack of concern, it proved to be a policy that soon gave cause for regret, not only to the Brethren of Trinity House but more so to the unfortunate and misguided citizens of Harwich. Instead of conspicuous lights, installed in prominent and well-found towers, they received only feeble and inefficient lights, displayed from two makeshift structures quite unsuited to the purpose, and barely able to meet the minimum requirements that the patent demanded. It was a state of affairs that the next hundred and fifty years did little to alter, and one which in the course of time rendered Harwich notorious for its antiquated system of lighting.

The Trinity Brethren, for their part, found to their dismay that they had been mistaken in their assumption. These were not after all to be regarded as local harbour lights but as major coastal beacons to which all vessels, whether entering Harwich or merely passing by at sea, would be required to contribute. The wording of the patent made that clear beyond all doubt:

> ". . . to be continually burning in the night season whereof Seafaring men and Mariners may take notice and avoid and escape the dangers, and ships the better come unto their harbours and ports without peril, and towards the maintenance of them certain Tolls and Duties payable *by all Ships passing or coming into that Harbour,* viz. Twelve pence on every twenty chaldrons of coals and one halfpenny per ton on English, and a penny per ton on foreign ships of other goods."

Sir William Batten was granted his patent on 24th December, 1664, an appropriate day for him to receive what Samuel Pepys likened to "the gift of a fortune."[8] Early in the New Year Sir William hastened off to Harwich to supervise the building of his lighthouses. Harwich was at this time a walled town with a principal gateway on the south side, through which the road from Colchester and London entered. This was the Town Gate, adjoining which

Sir William Batten's Harwich lights, with the former town gate appropriated to the use of a high lighthouse on the left. The low lighthouse is that provided by Isaac Leming Rebow in 1727, which is also the subject of the painting by John Constable on page 149.

was the Town Green extending to the water's edge. In a room above this gateway, with its large latticed window facing the sea, Sir William Batten contrived to set up his high lighthouse, installing a coal hearth with a ventilating pipe protruding through the roof to carry away the smoke. Two hundred yards away, at the seaward end of the Town Green, was erected a crude tower of timber, about twenty feet in height, to the summit of which was hoisted by night a lantern containing a single candle.

This much is evident from a description written shortly after the lights first came into use by Silas Taylor, who held the post of Keeper of the King's Stores at Harwich, in 1676. During his term of office Silas Taylor placed on record a wealth of information concerning Harwich and its history. Many years later these manuscripts came into the possession of another local historian, Samuel Dale, who published them in 1730, augmented by the results of his own researches.

"In a room over the Gate there is a Light kept all Night, blown by a fire of sea coals, which answer to a lesser and lower Light upon the Town Green. These two Lights brought together by Shipps from the Sea conduct them clear of the Andrews (a Sand stretching from Landguard Fort which makes, as it were, a bar across the entrance of the Harbour) into the Rolling Ground where there is good anchorage."[9]

The task of bringing his lights into service did not detain Sir William for long, and by the end of January, 1665, he was back in London where he was

143

taken suddenly and seriously ill. When Samuel Pepys came to record this fact in his diary on 7th February, he saw no reason to be hypocritical and made no attempt to mince his words:

> "This day Sir W. Batten, who hath been sick four or five days, is now very bad so as the people begin to fear his death; and I am at a loss whether it will be better for me to have him die because he is a bad man, or live for fear a worse should come."

Pepys could have saved himself this apprehension; Sir William in fact soon recovered, although this could well have been the first indication that his health had begun to fail him. A little over a year later, Pepys announced:

> "Sir W. Batten is come to town. I to see him; he is very ill of his fever and come only for advice."[10]

Four months later, on 5th October, comes the dramatic entry:

> "Much surprised with the news of the death of Sir W. Batten, who died this morning having been but two days sick."

A week later Pepys records that the body of Sir William had been taken to Walthamstow and buried in the parish church there, "an hundred or two of coaches attending his funeral." So passed Sir William Batten, after a long and distinguished career as an officer of the Navy, and a brief and uneventful one as proprietor of Harwich Lights.

Sir William was twice married. His first wife had died some years previously and was buried at Walthamstow, where the Battens had their country home. In February, 1659, Batten married Elizabeth Woodcock, of whose background we know nothing, beyond the fact that in August, 1661, Samuel Pepys went to Walthamstow and there heard some startling tales concerning the new Lady Batten; of how she had previously been someone else's whore, and of the dubious means by which she had come into her present estate. Reluctant at first to accept such gossip, Pepys eventually concluded that there must be something in it: "and indeed I do believe that the story is too true."[11] Now, more than six years later, this same Lady Batten found herself the chief beneficiary in her late husband's will, of which she was appointed an executrix. This responsibility was shared with one other executor, Sir John Barkman, otherwise Lord Leyenbergh.

The individual bequests contained in the will of Sir William Batten are of little interest here, except for those specifically concerned with the disposal of the lighthouses at Harwich. The profits from these were to be divided equally between Lady Batten and Sir William's five children. The lighthouses themselves were left in the custody of Mingo, his negro servant, whose dancing delighted the company assembled at the *Dolphin Inn* on more than one occasion. Of the six who were to share the revenue, three were married daughters whose portions immediately became the legal property of their respective husbands. In practice, then, only three of the nominated shareholders were beneficiaries in their own right. They were Lady Batten and Sir William's two sons, William and Benjamin. The others, whose entitlements came to them indirectly through marriage, were James Leming, husband of Mary Batten, Henry Askew, who was married to her sister Jane, and Jonathan Castle, who had recently married the plain and ageing Martha.[12] There is no way of knowing precisely how much a one-sixth share of the lights amounted to in terms of hard cash at this time, but it was evidently well worth having. John Whormby relates that in 1668 Lady Batten "out of a generosity to Navigation on account of her profits by the Harwich Lights" publicly offered to erect seamarks on the Naze to replace a conspicuous group of trees known as The Wrestlers which had become decayed.

For the first four years the profits were shared among the six original beneficiaries. Then, in 1671, Lady Batten married Lord Leyenbergh, the co-executor of her late husband's will. Leyenbergh was equally well known as Sir John Barkman, but neither name was strictly correct, for the gentleman was in reality Baron Hans Barikman Leijenbergh, Swedish envoy-extra-ordinary in London. He held this post for more than thirty years, during which time he lived at the Piazza in Covent Garden. His marriage to Lady Batten now gave him a rightful claim to her portion of the lighthouse shares. Both continued to discharge their duties as executors, although not very efficiently it seems, for in 1677 a Treasury Warrant was served on them demanding the sum of £60, representing twelve years arrears of rent on the lighthouses.[13]

The year 1671 brought other changes apart from the re-marriage of Lady Batten. In that year Sir William Batten's eldest daughter, Mary Leming, and her husband, James Leming, of Colchester, both died. There was an only child of their marriage, a daughter named Mary after her mother. The young Mary Leming was, in fact, the only grandchild of Sir William Batten and, as heiress to her parents' estate, now became the first of a new generation to benefit from the lights founded by her grandfather. The following year saw the death of another shareholder, Batten's elder son, William, whose portion was divided equally between the five surviving shareholders since he had no heir.

Meanwhile the lighthouses had become an established and familiar feature of the scene, tolerated only grudgingly by the citizens of Harwich, who felt that their town was being cheated out of a handsome source of profit. There had always been a strong contention among the local population that a substantial part of the income from the lights should be devoted to the good of the town, for the townspeople saw in this a ready means of providing for the paving and lighting of the streets and of financing the restoration work of which the parish church stood in such dire need. When Sir William Batten had begun to canvass support for his project, the majority had taken it for granted that Harwich stood to gain and had put their names somewhat impulsively to the petition in the firm belief that they were supporting a municipal move as much as a private venture. It may be true to say that Sir William Batten did nothing to foster this misunderstanding, but equally he did little to contradict it. Too late it was realised that this was a purely private enterprise over which the local corporation had no jurisdiction whatever. Now, after more than five years, the lights were yielding to their owners a clear annual profit which certainly ran into four figures, out of which Harwich waxed not a penny the richer, apart from the modest sum due to it in the form of rates.

There was nothing that could be done about it; the lights were the legal property of their owners, who held them under Letters Patent from the King and were answerable to no man. Nevertheless the Corporation of Harwich never gave up its efforts to secure some reversion of the revenue. No opportunity was missed to enlist the help of anyone with the initiative or sway to champion this cause, and it was an issue in which Samuel Pepys, as Member of Parliament for Harwich, inevitably, and to his cost, became involved.

Pepys' career in Parliament was perhaps the least successful of any aspect of his public life, being dogged throughout by malicious gossip and false charges. He was first elected to serve for the pocket borough of Castle Rising in Norfolk in 1673. He represented this constituency for nearly six years, during which time vicious rumours began to circulate, put about by those who were intent on bringing him down. He was, so they said, a Papist. A crucifix had been seen in his house, with statues and other symbols of Catholicism. There was even a suggestion that he had taken a hand in the Catholic plot to assassinate the King. All these allegations were later found to be without foundation, but the rumour-mongers had managed to throw enough mud to ensure that some would stick. In the eyes of the people of Castle Rising there was never smoke but there was fire, and when a general election came in 1679 Pepys had to look elsewhere for adoption. He turned to the seaports of Portsmouth and Harwich, and being successful at both, chose to take his seat for Harwich.

That particular Parliament lasted barely long enough to transact a single Bill, but by the time it had been dissolved and a new one elected in its place, Samuel Pepys lay in the Tower of London accused of Popery and treason. It was a different story entirely when the next election came in 1685. Cleared of the charges against him, Pepys again offered himself for election at Harwich, and was welcomed with open arms. He was, after all, a principal officer of the Navy Board, not to mention an Elder Brother and lately Master of Trinity House and Secretary of the Admiralty into the bargain. Many still remembered the clever ruse Pepys had devised for the defence of Harwich during the recent Dutch Wars. With an attack by the enemy fleet likely at any

Samuel Pepys, seen in a portrait painted
by John Closterman about 1695.
National Portrait Gallery

time, he had arranged for a wood and canvas imitation of the low light to be
set up in a false alignment relative to the high light. At the first sign of an
enemy ship, the real low light was to be demolished with high explosives,
leaving the high light and its mock companion to lure the Dutch fleet straight
on to the sands. It was a plan that had never had to be put to the test, but it
still remained fresh in the eyes of the electorate as polling day approached.
Here was a man who could evidently wield some authority over the owners of
the local lights. If anyone could succeed in the campaign to direct some of the
profits to the benefit of the town, it certainly ought to be him.

In electing Mr Pepys to represent them in Parliament, the citizens of
Harwich were confident that they were arming themselves with the biggest gun
they could lay hands on. To their dismay it misfired, Pepys making it plain
from the outset that he could do nothing in the matter of the local lights. The
existing grant still had more than forty years to run, and while it remained
valid neither the Corporation of Harwich, Trinity House, nor even Parliament
itself had any power to interfere. It was an attitude that the constituency found
hard to accept. Samuel Pepys, who only needed to utter a word of command
for the lighthouses to be blown sky-high, was now asking them to believe that
in matters of finance he was powerless to touch a single penny piece. It took a
bit of swallowing. Pepys stood again for Harwich in the election of 1689, but it
was evident from the start that he was no longer the popular figure that he had
been previously. His constituents were clearly disappointed by his failure to
take up an issue which they regarded as being of paramount importance. If

Samuel Pepys would not support their endeavours, then perhaps somebody else would. Like the people of Castle Rising before them they had reasons for wishing him to be gone, and like the people of Castle Rising they seized on the same excuse of Popery. It had the desired effect; the election resulted in a sweeping victory for the opposition and Samuel Pepys finished at the bottom of the poll.

It marked the end of his career, not only in politics but in public life. Within weeks he resigned his post at the Admiralty and retired. He spent the fourteen years that remained to him living in obscurity while he worked on his projected *History of the Navy* but, alas for posterity, he never lived to bring the work into print.

Two years after Pepys took his leave of Harwich, the shareholders in the local lights were reduced to four by the death of Lord Leyenbergh. The former Lady Batten had died in 1681 and was buried beside her first husband at Walthamstow.[14] Both her marriages had been without children and now, with the passing of Lord Leyenbergh, this portion was divided among the four surviving shareholders. Of these, the key figure proved to be the young heiress, Mary Leming. By her marriage to Isaac Rebow, of Colchester, the Harwich lights became associated with one of the most respected and influential families in the county of Essex.

The Rebows came to Colchester with the influx of weavers from the Low Countries. From modest beginnings they prospered by the production of the fine-weave cloths known as says and bays and perpetuanas which found a ready market in the mediterranean countries and for which Colchester became justly renowned. The father figure of the family seems to have been John Rebow, who by the year 1685 had become wealthy enough to purchase Colchester castle. He married Sarah, daughter of Francis Tayspill, of Colchester, by whom he had a son and heir, Isaac, born in 1658. It was this Isaac who married Mary Leming and thus became possessed of her share in the lighthouses. Isaac Rebow became an even more prominent citizen than his father, and in due course held the offices of High Steward of Essex and Recorder of Colchester, in addition to representing that town in ten successive parliaments. He stood in high favour with William III, who was a frequent guest at Rebow's house in Head Street. It was here, on 27th March, 1693, that Rebow was knighted by his royal visitor.[15]

In 1696 Sir William Batten's original lease passed the half-way mark and there occurred one of those sudden subversive moves to which the owner of any lighthouse was always prone. Quite unexpectedly there came before the Privy Council an application from a certain Sir Francis Compton for a licence to continue the lighthouses for a further thirty-one years after the current lease terminated.[16] It may seem strange that this request should have come more than thirty years in advance, from someone totally unconnected with the existing lease, and stranger still, perhaps, that it should have come almost to the point of being granted. Sir Francis Compton, however, was on fairly secure ground. As an official of the Treasury Office he was in a position to know the precise details of this and every other grant, including the length of time still to come in the current term. In 1678 he had been one of seven appointed to serve under the Earl of Peterborough in the capacity of Receivers of Ancient Revenues.[17]

The application succeeded in getting so far as for the Treasury Office to be asked for particulars of the existing rents and receipts in order that the details of a new grant to Sir Francis Compton could be worked out. Nobody at the Treasury seemed to know precisely what these details were, so the matter was referred to the Surveyor-General of Crown Lands. He was not sure either, and in a report to the Treasury dated 24th April, 1696, he was obliged to admit:

> "I have no certain account in my office of the profits arising by these lighthouses, but by enquiring and comparing these duties with what is paid for other lighthouses on the same coast, they seem to be worth about £700 per annum and I therefore rate the desired lease at £1,750."[18]

This represented nearly six times the sum currently being charged, and it may well have proved too much for Sir Francis, for nothing more seems to have come of the affair.

Exactly ten years elapsed before the question of renewing the lease was raised again. All the shareholders of the older generation were now dead and their shares had become widely dispersed among various distant relatives. Of

A painting by John Constable showing the front lighthouse at Harwich built by Isaac Leming Rebow in 1727.   *The Tate Gallery*

the four remaining portions only one was still in the hands of a direct descendant, Sir Isaac Rebow. He and his wife, Lady Mary, once the juniors among the original shareholders, were now the seniors among a new generation of owners. This meant that Sir Isaac was more favourably placed than anyone else to seek a renewal of the grant. Accordingly, in 1707, he submitted a petition showing that he was entitled to a fourth part of the lighthouses erected by Sir William Batten near Harwich through his marriage with a granddaughter of the said Sir William Batten, and therefore praying that he might be granted a further term on expiration of the current lease.[19]

Sir Isaac's application was in his own name only, so if it was successful the others would be eliminated, leaving him in receipt of the sole benefit. No precise number of years was specified in this petition and the Treasury Office referred the case to the Surveyor of Crown Lands for his advice as to how long a term should be granted. Sir Francis Compton's abortive request had been for thirty-one years, made at a time when the term in being stood at thirty years, and would therefore have restored the grant to its original duration of sixty-one years. The Surveyor-General recommended that this grant to Sir Issac Rebow should be on the same basis of a thirty-one years extension, making the lease terminable in 1756 as would have been the case with Sir Francis Compton. Not content with this, Sir Isaac petitioned again in 1714 and was successful in obtaining a further grant of sixty-one years to commence when the extension came to an end in 1756. This put the lighthouses securely in the hands of the Rebow family until 1817.

When Sir Isaac Rebow died in September, 1726, his only son, Leming Rebow, had been dead for nine years, so the family fortunes passed into the hands of his grandson, Isaac Leming Rebow. During the first year of his ownership, Isaac Leming Rebow undertook to replace the Harwich front light with a more substantial structure, the first attempt at alteration or improvement to have been made throughout the sixty years that the lights had been in service. The new tower was a square structure of overlapped planking with a fixed lantern in place of the former hoistable one in which "are set up every night six great candles each weighing one pound."[20]

Isaac Leming Rebow married Mary, daughter of Matthew Martin, of Wivenhoe, and their son, Isaac Martin Rebow, succeeded to the Rebow estates in 1735. The new owner was to remain in possession for the next 46 years. The most important happening during this time took place at Christmas, 1764, when the front light was changed from candles to oil. Subsequent accounts show that it took between seventy and eighty gallons a year to keep the low light in commission.

Isaac Martin Rebow died in 1781, leaving his entire estate to his only daughter, Mary Hesther Rebow. So, for the second time in their history, Harwich lights became the property of a sole heiress, it having been through the marriage of an earlier heiress, Mary Leming, that the patent had come to the Rebows in the first place. The future now depended upon whether or not Mary Hesther were to marry, for if she did the lights would be delivered into the hands of another family altogether. At first there appeared every prospect that she would remain single, and for the next fifteen years Mary Hesther enjoyed the sole benefit of the revenue.

The Rebows had by now reached the peak of their prosperity. The family seat had moved from Colchester to Wivenhoe Hall, an estate purchased from the Beriff family. It had formerly been the seat of the Earls of Oxford, who had maintained its great gateway as a mark for ships entering the River Colne. Here the Rebows lived and flourished, adding to their other thriving interests the operation of a fleet of sailing vessels bearing their various names in the Mediterranean fruit trade. Mary Hesther's sole ownership came to an end in 1796 when she married Colonel Francis Slater, of Chesterfield. This did not dissociate the lights from the name with which they had now been connected for over a hundred years, however, for shortly after the marriage Colonel Slater, by deed poll, added the name of Rebow to his own.

The rank of Colonel was no meaningless courtesy title. Francis Slater Rebow was a serving army officer who spent much time abroad with his regiment, leaving his business affairs at home to his agent and legal advisor. In 1809, with the lighthouse lease within eight years of terminating, he was persuaded personally to seek a renewal of the grant. His petition sparked off the most protracted and fiercely-contested fight for a lighthouse since Sir John Meldrum's battle for Winterton two hundred years previously. For more than six years the proceedings dragged on, bringing proposal and objection, counter-proposal and counter-objection. Opposition came from three separate quarters. Trinity House of London was intent on laying claim to what was rightfully its own, its counterparts at Newcastle and Hull acted in the interests of the English coasting trade, and the ever-hopeful Corporation of Harwich, after all these years, still cherished the ambition to acquire the revenue.

All this took place during the period of the Napoleonic Wars when Slater Rebow, with the rank of Major-General, was abroad on active service. Despite this, his agent wrote him an urgent letter advising him to obtain special leave of absence that he might return home to conduct his bid to retain ownership of the lights personally. This General Rebow did, and after much persuasion the Lords of the Treasury came to the point of recommending that his petition should be granted. Renewed protests came from London Trinity House, who declared that they could never agree to a renewal in favour of any private individual. They estimated that General Rebow's income from the lights amounted to about £5,000 a year with all expenses met, in return for two lights which still stood much as they had been built a century and a half earlier. The high light was still a coal fire, shining through the latticed window of an upper

room, obscured by soot and bedevilled by smoke, while the new low light was structurally identical to its predecessor apart from its fixed lantern which had replaced the former hoistable one. The Lords of the Treasury took note of these arguments and made it a condition of the renewal, firstly, that General Rebow should build two new towers and install in them more up to date equipment, and, secondly, he would in future be required to surrender to the Crown three-fifths of the nett profits. General Rebow eventually agreed to these stringent terms and in 1815 received an extension for thirty-one years commencing from 5th January, 1817.

Work on the new lighthouses began early in 1817. The towers were built alongside, and in the same line of direction as, the ones they replaced. They were octagonal in shape, and extensive use was made of white brick in their construction. The high lighthouse was carried to a height of more than 70 feet to make it conspicuous by day, although the actual light was situated only half way up the tower in order to retain the same elevation as at the former high light. The low light was a scaled down version of the high light, from which it was separated by a distance of 218 yards. The completed tower stood just over 30 feet with the light at an elevation of 25 feet to match its predecessor.

The high lighthouse, with nine oil burners and reflectors, and the low light with three similar lamps, could now be seen over a far greater distance than the former lights. Even now, however, the disadvantages of the old lights

Opposite: A mid-nineteenth century engraving of General Rebow's high lighthouse.
Colchester Central Library

Right: The low lighthouse as General Rebow built it in 1817, before addition of the "umbrella" canopy to make it into a sea-front shelter.
Colchester Central Library

were not completely overcome. An inherent weakness of the original lights had been the minimal difference in their respective elevations (the high light exceeded the low by a mere five feet) which made them appear as one light when seen at a distance. In the past this problem had not been over-serious since it was not too difficult to distinguish between the uneven flicker of the high light's coal fire and the steady glow of the single oil lamp at the low light, but now the high light was three times more powerful than the low and completely eclipsed it. Serious complaints began to be made of difficulties in keeping the lights in line when approaching the harbour. In an attempt to avoid further confusion it was announced that as from 1st February, 1819, the colour of the low light would be changed to red. Even this did not remedy the situation altogether and it came to be realised that the only way to eradicate the trouble entirely was to ensure that the two lights were more widely and positively separated. In May, 1822, the following announcement was made:

NOTICE TO MARINERS—HARWICH LIGHTS

As from 13th May 1822 the Light at the High Lighthouse will be exhibited from the Upper Floor of that Tower instead of its present situation and will be thenceforward continued every night from Sunset to Sunrise as usual.

At the same time the opportunity was taken to increase the number of lamps from nine to ten, thereby giving the high light an effective range of thirteen miles under clear conditions. These alterations at last produced the desired effect and the lights were continued in this form throughout the remaining forty years of their existence.

The grant of thirty-one years to General Rebow in 1817 ran, in the event, for only nineteen years, until Parliament put an end to the private ownership of lighthouses in 1836. Under the terms of this legislation agreement was reached with General Rebow for his interests in the Harwich lights to be transferred to the Corporation of Trinity House as from 1st January, 1837, the amount paid in compensation for the twelve years and five days unexpired portion of the lease amounting in total to £160,076.[21] This figure comprised £31,730 personal compensation to General Rebow and £128,346 for the interests of the Crown. Although this was by any standards a formidable sum, it fell far short of the £300,000 that the Spurn lights had cost or the £444,000 paid for the Skerries.

Of all the private concessions bought out by Trinity House, Harwich proved within a short time to be the least successful and the most costly. A few years after being taken over the lights were rendered useless by coastal erosion. They were by no means the only lighthouses to be put out of action in this manner, but ironically the trouble in this case was entirely of man's own making. It happened that the material in the cliffs in the immediate vicinity of Harwich and Felixstowe had the peculiar property of petrifying when exposed to the air. In this state sections could be dug out and ground down to provide a highly efficient bonding agent for building. This was no new discovery; the possibilities had been realised since the earliest times, and the fact that the powdered-down substance went by the name of Roman cement is indicative of how long it had been in use. An early example of its employment on a large scale was in the building of the walls and gateways surrounding the town of Harwich, Daniel Defoe being prompted to remark on this during his visit in 1722:

> "They boast that their town is walled and their streets paved with clay, yet one is as strong and the other as clean as those that are paved with stone."[6]

Early in the nineteenth century these resources began to be tapped on a large scale. Huge inroads were made into Cobbold's Point on the Felixstowe side of the harbour and massive quantities of shingle began to build up round the tip of Landguard Point, creating what is technically termed a "pocket beach". Normally this would have been neutralised by the scouring action of the tide, but similar excavation of the rock from Beacon Cliff at Harwich effectively widened the harbour mouth, slowing down the tidal current so that the shingle deposits from Landguard Point were no longer swept away. In the space of thirty years the point grew out by about 500 yards and in the channel, which was formerly more than forty feet deep at low water, there was now a shingle ridge projecting as many feet above high tide mark. Worse still, an area of shallow now lay right across the line of direction indicated by the lighthouses, earning for them the dubious title of "The Misleading Lights of Harwich".

In 1843, following the presentation of a memorial by the Corporation of Harwich to the Admiralty, a survey was carried out by Captain John Washington, in command of the naval vessel *Shearwater*. Captain Washington, later to become Rear-Admiral and Hydrographer of the Navy, made his report to the Secretary of the Admiralty on 19th January, 1843.

"The port of Harwich, owing to its great depth of water, its extent, the shelter it affords and its immediate communication with the sea, is one of the most valuable on our eastern shores, and although the Rivers Thames and Humber afford shelter by running far up them, yet Harwich from its easy access by night or day, in all weather and in all states of the tide is the only harbour of refuge, properly so called, on the East Coast of England.

The memorial of the Mayor and other inhabitants of the Borough of Harwich states that in this harbour, which in easterly gales has given shelter to 500 sail of shipping at once, great changes have taken place within the last 20 years owing to the falling down of Beacon Cliff on the Western side of the entrance and the growing out of Landguard Point on the Eastern side, whereby the harbour is already much deteriorated and is daily becoming worse.

To the truth of this statement I can bear the fullest testimony from my own observations during the last two years, and all the evidence I can obtain goes to show the sole immediate cause of the damage in question is the digging up and carrying away the cement stone from the foot of Beacon Cliff to Felixstowe Ledge."

From details given by Captain Washington it appears that in the fifty years beginning in 1706 the cliff line was cut back by some 40 feet. During the next fifty years this figure increased to 120 feet, while during the remaining thirty-seven years up to the time of his report the cliff fell back by no less than 350 feet. The report continued:

"This mischief has been accelerated by the carrying away the cement stone from the foot of Felixstowe cliff about 2½ miles to the north-eastward where it formed a rocky projecting ledge which served as a breakwater for the whole shore from the force of the sea in north-easterly gales. But since this stone has been removed (to an extent of 200,000 tons I am told) a large slice of Felixstowe cliff has gone into the sea, 2 Martello towers and a small battery only built in 1808 have been swept away, and the beach at Landguard Point has grown out to the extent of 500 yards, in consequence of which the two lighthouses erected but a few years since at a great expense are no longer a safe leading mark into the harbour; on the contrary they have already caused serious damage to several vessels by running them ashore."[22]

There was, unfortunately, no way of reversing the changes that had already taken place, so the southerly extension of Landguard Point had to be accepted as a permanency.

In 1858 a revolutionary design of lighthouse, built on tubular metal legs driven down through the sea bed into the hard strata beneath, first made its appearance. The upper ends projected high above the water and were braced and stayed with iron tie-rods to form a firm structure on which the lighthouse buildings could be raised, with the whole surmounted by the lantern. When completed it resembled a house on stilts, which, indeed it was, and the nature of the design suited it particularly to locations that were awash all or part of the time, such as sandbanks and foreshores. Known as the Mitchell Screwpile Lighthouse, its strength lay in its lack of resistance to wind and waves. In the course of time it came to be made great use of by the Americans along their

The screw pile lighthouses at Dovercourt which took over from the Harwich "misleading lights" in 1863, seen when they were in operation. The Dovercourt lights were discontinued in 1917.

The Harwich high light as one of the country's most unusual dwellings.

Atlantic sea coast. The first of them was brought into service by Trinity House on the Maplin Sands near Shoeburyness in 1858 and, it having proved itself satisfactory in all respects, it was decided to make use of the same design as a replacement for the Harwich lights.

A pair of these lighthouses was now set up on the foreshore at Dovercourt, about a mile to the south of Harwich. The upper lighthouse was positioned at the back of the beach above high water mark, while the smaller front light was situated out beyond the tide-line. The two were connected by a concrete causeway which remained dry except for a brief period when the tide was near to full. Lighting was by oil lamps with silver-plated reflectors, showing a fixed or steady light. When brought into line they led further to the south than Harwich lights had done and vessels were thereby drawn well clear of the tip of Landguard Point. At daybreak on 2nd November, 1863, Harwich lights were extinguished for good and at dusk that same evening the new lights at Dovercourt were kindled.

So ended the tradition of sea lights displayed from Harwich which had continued unbroken for almost 200 years. Their successors at Dovercourt had a comparatively brief and uneventful life. The high light of the pair was improved in May 1878, when a prismatic lens was installed in place of the parabolic reflectors, and soon after 1900 both lighthouses were converted to gas lighting, the high light being given a flashing character.

In 1917 Harwich Harbour Board took over from Trinity House responsibility for the approaches to Harwich and immediately marked the passage into the harbour with a series of lighted buoys. This rendered the lights at Dovercourt redundant and in August, 1917, they were discontinued after fifty-four years in service.

The disused towers of both pairs of lights remain. At Dovercourt the two screwpile structures stand with their feet firmly planted in the seabed, their upper works betraying the effects of more than sixty years of corrosion and neglect. One day a decision will have to be taken on whether they should be allowed to stand or fall; the second option could well turn out to be more costly and troublesome than the first. General Rebow's towers at Harwich are in a more fortunate state. In 1969 the old front tower received a new lease of life when it was converted to a depot for Trinity House pilots, but after ten years in this role it became redundant again with the completion of a new pilots' headquarters alongside the Trinity House depot and it now houses a small maritime museum. The high lighthouse became a private residence in 1909, but later came on the market and was at long last acquired by the local Corporation. If only their predecessors could have lived to see the day! For several years following the Second World War the former lighthouse stood empty, being advertised to let at one stage for the attractive sum of £1 per week. In 1975 it received due recognition as a building worthy of care and preservation and at the suggestion of the Colchester branch of the Royal Institute of British Architects, in association with the local archaeological society, was renovated as a contribution to European Architectural Heritage year.

Harwich low light during the time it was serving as a Trinity House pilot station. It now houses a small maritime museum assembled largely by the efforts of the Harwich lifeboat crew.

Postscript

(Latter day events)

DESPITE its ancient ties, its deep-rooted traditions and a certain preoccupation with pomp and ceremony, today's Trinity House could never be accused of living in the past. The activities of its experimental station at Dungeness portend the future in the same way that the ceremonial frock coats of its Elder Brethren recall the past.

Since 1836 the Corporation has existed as an authority rather than a monopoly, but despite the widely-held contention that such bodies breed apathy and inefficiency the coast lighting throughout the Trinity House area of jurisdiction is acknowledged to be second to none among the maritime nations of the world. The years between the turn of the present century and the start of the Second World War saw the coast lights of England and Wales reach their maximum numbers. This was particularly so in the case of manned lightvessels, most of which were deployed among the shoal waters off East Anglia and in the Thames approaches. This sector was administered by two Trinity House depots, one at Harwich and the other at Great Yarmouth. Between them they controlled twenty-seven lightvessels and twenty-two lighthouses reaching from the Forelands of Kent to Withernsea on the coast of Yorkshire. The lighthouses included eleven Thames river lights and four screwpile lighthouses in the outer Thames approaches.

With oil, or any other illuminant requiring frequent attention, automation was out of the question and the only economies possible were the complete withdrawal of any light that proved superfluous. These chapters have already shown that Hunstanton and Winterton were early casualties in 1921. Electricity not only brought a more efficient light-source, it permitted the development of the time-switch, which led first to partial and ultimately to total automation. Lowestoft and Southwold lighthouses were electrified and semi-automated in 1938, but further progress was temporarily halted by the outbreak of war in the following year.

On 11th January, 1940, the Smith's Knoll lightvessel was savagely attacked by an enemy aircraft. It was not an isolated incident, and before long other North Sea lightships found themselves sitting ducks for stray German aircrews out for some casual target practice. Except for the Cork, close in to Felixstowe, all the lightships were taken off station and spent much of the remainder of the war years moored in Sea Reach in the Thames.

When peace returned the work of research and development was resumed, with the result that in the late nineteen-sixties a new type of high

The Inner Dowsing light tower, which has replaced a lightship on this station.

Trinity House

focal plane automatic buoy made its appearance. It enabled the Corton lightship to be dispensed with in 1968 and the Kentish Knock in 1975.

Like most large organisations, Trinity House had to make concessions to the push-button age, and in some respects it was a pioneer in the field of automation. It was one of the first to perfect mechanisms sufficiently robust and reliable to function remotely and unceasingly for months at a time. Automation is normally an economy measure aimed at cutting costs by reducing the staff on the payroll. Trinity House was less concerned with costs than with posts, which it was finding ever more difficult to fill due to the demanding and anti-social nature of the work involved. As jobs ashore became more plentiful and pay scales more attractive, fewer personnel leaving the Navy or the trawler fleets, traditional recruiting grounds for Trinity House, were prepared to be incarcerated for weeks on end in a stone tower or be buffetted night and day aboard a ship that went nowhere.

Early in the nineteen-seventies there began a fundamental reorganisation of the Trinity House district depots and the means employed to relieve keepers and crews. It was decided to use helicopters to ferry personnel to and from lightships and rock stations. This left the fleet of tenders free to concentrate on carrying supplies and to engage in buoy maintenance, wreck marking and a host of other routine duties. With double manning of the tenders the fleet was reduced from nine vessels to five. The new arrangements soon made themselves outwardly apparent. Lightvessels began to sprout helicopter landing pads over their stern quarters, while famous lighthouses such as the Bishop Rock and Eddystone took on a mushroom appearance as these circular superstructures spread a canopy above them. But any loss of grace and outline was more than compensated for by the speed and regularity with which keepers and crews could be relieved, regardless of weather conditions. No longer were there heard the once-familiar news reports of lightkeepers

A diagram of the Large Automatic Navigation Buoy (LANBY) which has replaced three lightvessels off the East Anglian coast.

Trinity House

LARGE AUTOMATIC NAVIGATION BUOY
LANBY 200 SERIES No. 201-209

A Telemetry aerial
B Racon
C Main and Standby lights
D Emergency light
E Bearing light
F Anchor light
G Fog signal
H Emergency fog signal
J Intake and Exhaust ducts
K Entrance door
L Equipment hatches
M Fuelling hatches
N 3 point Mooring lugs
P Mooring chain

Height of focal plane
above water line.................12.2 metres
Diameter of hull...................12.2 metres
Depth of hull.....................2.3 metres
Weight of buoy :–   Empty........55 tonnes
        Normal water ballast........25 tonnes
                Max. fuel load........15 tonnes
                        Total........95 tonnes

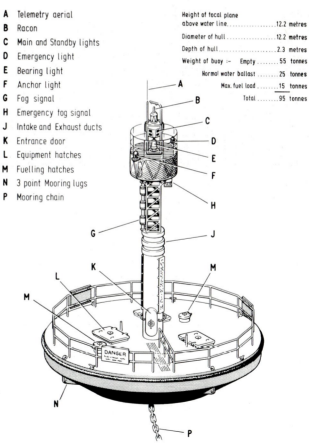

being brought ashore at the end of January to celebrate with their families a Christmas which the rest of the world had already forgotten.

Another product of this period was the Large Automatic Navigational Buoy, or LANBY, as it was dubbed by an acronymic age. These giant buoys, forty feet in diameter and weighing eighty tons apiece, represented the nearest approach so far to a robot lightvessel. In addition to the light they incorporated an electric fog-horn and a radar beacon, and were capable of being remotely operated and monitored from a nearby lightship or base depot. Three of them soon made their appearance off the East Anglian coast, replacing the Lynn Well, Cross Sand and Cork lightvessels.

A further effect of this restructuring was the downgrading of the Great Yarmouth depot to become a sub-depot of Harwich. In its heyday Yarmouth controlled all the lightvessels and lighthouses along a coastal sector extending from Southwold to Withernsea. In the main this activity now switched to Harwich, although the Yarmouth buoy yard and workshops are still retained.

In April, 1977, work began on changing the entire buoyage system in home waters to bring it into line with the standards agreed by the International Association of Lighthouse Authorities. By 1981 this change-over was almost total throughout the coasts of Europe.

So, after a decade of transition, the lights of East Anglia were brought to their present disposition. Between Harwich harbour and the mouth of the Wash stand five lighthouses, among which only Cromer is continually watched, and plans are already well advanced for this to become a man and wife station. Offshore within the same boundaries the number of manned lightvessels stands at four. The most recent vessel to be withdrawn was the Shipwash, taken out of service in June, 1981, when its place was taken by a completely automatic lightship, the first of its kind, monitored from the base depot at Harwich. Every twenty-eight days a Trinity House helicopter lifts off from a helipad in front of Cromer lighthouse to relieve the Dudgeon, Dowsing and Humber lightvessels and the Inner Dowsing fixed platform. A similar mission is flown from the North Denes airfield at Caister to the Haisbro, Newarp and Smith's Knoll lightships.

Nowadays, when navigational aids are based on radio waves rather than light beams, doubts are sometimes expressed over whether the future still holds a place for the lighted seamark. The fact is that however effective modern electronic systems may be, and regardless of how sophisticated they may yet become, they are nothing more than aids to navigation, just as lights and seamarks are aids. Each has its limitations; neither can hope to be totally foolproof and therefore the one must exist in support of the other. This being so, it is highly unlikely that the coast of East Anglia, which witnessed the birth of lights and seamarks, or indeed the coasts of Great Britain as a whole, will ever be allowed to fall into darkness again.

Appendix of Sources and References

INTRODUCTION

1. *The Trades Increase.* Robert Kayle (1615).
2. *Plan of the English Commerce.* Daniel Defoe (1716).
3. *Norfolk Archeology* Vol. IV (1855).
4. *An Act touching Seamarks and Mariners.* (Anno octavo Reginae Elizabethae) (1566).
5. Hist. MSS Commission (Finch) Vol. III.
6. Report of the Select Committee on Foreign Trade (1822).
7. *An Act for Vesting Lighthouses Lights and Seamarks on the Coasts of England and Wales in the Corporation of Trinity House.* (VI and VII William IV, 1836).

CROMER

1. *Great Britain's Coasting Pilot.* Captain Greenville Collins, London (1685).
2. *Antiquities of Middlesex.* John Bowack, London (1705).
3. Rebecca Clayton married Sir Robert Paston of Oxnead Hall near Buxton in Norfolk.
4. Calendar of State Papers (Domestic Series) 1669-70.
5. Cal. State Papers (Dom) 1673 p. 41.
6. Norfolk and Norwich Record Office MS 14666.
7. Cal. State Papers (Dom) 1674 p. 457.
8. Trinity House Court Minutes 3.12.1718.
9. In the composition of Ipswich Corporation the dignity of Portman roughly equated to that of an Alderman. Edward Bowell was Bailiff of Ipswich for the years 1723 and 1729.
10. Public Record Office PROB 11/686 f. 240.
11. Trinity House Court Minutes 22.4.1719.
12. Report of the Royal Commission on Lighthouses (1861).
13. The other was St Agnes, Isles of Scilly.
14. The Norfolk Tour, 1819.
15. *Cromer Considered as a Watering Place.* Edmund Bartell.
16. *Norfolk Chronicle* 3.12.1866.
17. *Cromer—Past and Present.* Walter Rye. Jarrold (1889).

WINTERTON

1. Trinity House transcripts, 1609-1625.
2. Norfolk and Norwich Record Office MS 15995.
3. John Meldrum was not knighted until 6th August, 1622.
4. *The Answer of the Masters of Trinitie House to the Special Objection of the Patentees for the Keeping of Winterton Lights.* Norfolk and Norwich Record Office.
5. *Tracts Relating to the Army and Navy,* Vol. 7. State Papers Room, British Library.
6. Trinity House Court Minutes 22.8.1677.
7. Trinity House Court Minutes 25.8.1677.
8. Trinity House Court Minutes 1.9.1677.
9. Trinity House Select Entries 17.2.1683.
10. Trinity House Court Minutes 24.4.1683.

11. Sir Edward Turnour, the elder, was appointed a Younger Brother of Trinity House on 14th October, 1665.
12. Turnour MSS (uncatalogued). Norfolk and Norwich Record Office.
13. *An Account of Trinity House and of Seamarks in General* by John Whormby, Clerk of the said Corporation, London (1861).
14. A floating light was ultimately established at the Cockle Sand in 1843.
15. Report of the Royal Commission on Lighthouses (1861).
16. *Victoria County History of Suffolk,* Vol. II.
17. Norfolk and Norwich Record Office Map ERS 4193(255).

ORFORD NESS

1. Cal. State Papers (Dom.) 1634/35.
2. Historical Manuscripts Commission, Vol. IV.
3. *Survey of England's Champions.* Josiah Ricraft (1647).
4. *The Early History of the Merchant Taylor's Company.* C. M. Clode, London (1888).
5. *History of Tottenham.* Bedwell (1631).
6. Public Record Office MSS c66/2980 No. 2.
7. Norfolk and Norwich Record Office. MS 10082/35E2.
8. Turnour Correspondence. West Sussex Record Office.
9. Calendar of Treasury Papers. Vol. X. p. 371.
10. Calendar of Treasury Books 3.5.1695.
11. Calendar of Treasury Papers 7.6.1695.
12. Turnour Correspondence. West Sussex Record Office.
13. Turnour Correspondence. West Sussex Record Office.
14. Historical Manuscripts Commission, Portland MSS Vol. 7.
15. Turnour Correspondence. West Sussex Record Office.
16. Pepys' Diary. 27.2.1662.
17. Report of the Royal Commission on Lighthouses. (1861).

LOWESTOFT

1. *Tracts Relating to the Army and Navy,* Vol. 7, f. 16. State Papers Room, British Library.
2. Pepys' Diary. 10.9.1663.
3. *Pepys' Naval Minutes.* The Navy Records Society (1926).
4. In defending his seat at Harwich in the election of 1689.
5. Trinity House Court Minutes, 25.5.1676.
6. *London Gazette.* 16.10.1676.
7. Calendar of State Papers (Dom.) 1676 p. 270.
8. Calendar of State Papers (Dom.) 1676 p. 33.
9. Calendar of Treasury Books 13.1.1682.
10. *Pepys' Naval Minutes.* The Navy Records Society (1926).
11. *Ipswich Journal* 21.12.1770.
12. *Town and Country Magazine,* June 1778.
13. *The World's Lighthouses Before 1820.* D. Alan Stevenson. Oxford University Press (1959).
14. *The History of the Lowestoft Lighthouses.* W. R. Chaplin. Unpublished typescript in Trinity House Library, 1959.
15. *London Gazette.* 19.1.1782.

16. *An Historic Account of the Ancient Town of Lowestoft.* Edmund Arthur Gillingwater (1790).
17. Entry in log book. T.H.V. *Vestal* 1841.
18. James Douglass, builder of the Wolf Rock, Bishop's Rock and Eddystone lighthouses, among others.
19. *London Gazette.* December 1880.

HUNSTANTON

1. "Float" was the old-fashioned term for a lightvessel.
2. The narrow lane leading from Old Hunstanton village to the main road is still known locally as Chapel Bank.
3. *A Tour through the Eastern Counties.* Daniel Defoe.
4. King's Lynn Corporation archives.
5. Trinity House Court Minutes 16.10.1663.
6. King's Lynn Corporation archives.
7. *An Account of Trinity House and of Seamarks in General,* by John Whormby, Clerk of the said Corporation (1746).
8. *History of Hunstanton Lighthouse.* Calvert. Jarrolds, 1939.
9. King's Lynn Corporation archives.
10. Trinity House Court Minutes. 7.9.1710.
11. The grant of Anne, anno IX 27.2.1711.
12. The grant of 25th George II 31.10.1751.
13. The precise cost was £859.76.
14. *History of King's Lynn.* Richards.
15. This was the "spangle light" at Lowestoft.
16. King's Lynn Corporation archives.
17. "Returns to Orders of the Honourable House of Commons" (Certified at the Trinity House 16th February 1826).
18. The Lynn Well lightvessel was replaced by an automatic buoy in September, 1973.
19. *Victoria County History of Suffolk,* Vol. II.
20. Report of the Royal Commission on Lighthouses (1861).
21. The original draft is in the author's possession.

HARWICH

1. *Pepys' Naval Minutes.* The Navy Records Society (1926).
2. Charles II once told Samuel Pepys that Sir William Batten's new ketch must have been of his own getting, so broad was its beam when compared to its length. Diary 21.4.1666.
3. Calendar of State Papers (Dom.) 19.9.1638.
4. Pepys' Diary 15.11.1665.
5. Pepys' Diary 17.6.1664.
6. *A Tour Through the Whole Island of Great Britain.* Daniel Defoe (1722).
7. Trinity House Court Minutes 2.11.1664.
8. *Pepys' Naval Minutes.* The Navy Records Society (1926).
9. *A History of Harwich and Dovercourt.* Samuel Dale (1730).
10. Pepys' Diary 28.6.1667.
11. Pepys' Diary 1.8.1661.

12. It was this same Martha Batten whom Pepys made his Valentine—"which I do only out of complacency." Diary 14.2.1660.
13. Calendar of Treasury Papers Vol. V. p. 911.
14. *The Environs of London.* Lysons.
15. *Victoria County History of Essex.*
16. Calendar of Treasury Books Vol. XI (1695/96).
17. Calendar of Treasury Papers 23.1.1677/78.
18. Calendar of Treasury Books Vol. XI (1696/97. p. 109).
19. Calendar of Treasury Papers 9.2.1706/07.
20. *History of Essex.* Morant (1768).
21. Report of the Royal Commission on Lighthouses (1861).
22. Report of the Royal Commission on East Coast Harbours and Refuges. State Papers Room, British Library.

Bibliography

In addition to the titles specifically quoted in the Appendix of Sources and References, the following works were consulted during research:

GENERAL

The Physical Geography of the Oceans. Charles H. Cotter. American Elsevier Publishing Co. Inc., New York 1966.
The North Sea. George Morey. Frederick Muller, London 1968.
Coals from Newcastle. Roger Finch. Terence Dalton, Lavenham 1973.
British Maps and Map-makers. Edward Lyneham. Collins, London 1944.
The Sea Coast. J. A. Steers. Collins, London 1969.
Trinity House. Hilary P. Mead. Sampson Low, London 1947.
Trinity House of Deptford. G. G Harris. University of London The Athlone Press 1969.
Lighthouses—A Rudimentary Treatise. A. Stevenson. London 1850.
Lighthouses. D. Stevenson. Adam & Charles Black, Edinburgh 1864.
Lighthouses and Lightships. F. A. Talbot. William Heinemann, London 1913.
British Lighthouses. J. P. Bowen. Published for the British Council, Longman Green, London 1946.
English Lighthouse Tours. D. Alan Stevenson. Nelson, London 1946.
Samuel Pepys—The Man in the Making. Sir Arthur Bryant. Collins, London (1933).
Samuel Pepys—The Years of Peril. Sir Arthur Bryant. Collins, London (1935).
Samuel Pepys—Saviour of the Navy. Sir Arthur Bryant. Collins, London (1938).
Samuel Pepys and the Royal Navy. J. R. Tanner. Cambridge University Press, 1920.
The Life of Daniel Defoe. Thomas Wright. Cassell (1894).
The Incredible Defoe. William Freeman. Herbert Jenkins, London 1950.

REGIONAL

History and Antiquities of the Seignory of Holderness. G. Poulson. Vol. 1 (1840) Vol. 2 (1841). Robert Brown, Hull.
The Lost Towns of the Yorkshire Coast. T. Shepperd. A. Brown, Hull 1912.
East Anglia. J. E. Ritchie. Jarrold, London 1893.
East Anglia—England's Eastern Province. R. H. Mottram. Chapman Hall, London 1933.
Eastern England. John Bygott. George Routledge, London 1923.
Norfolk and Suffolk. W. G. Clarke. A. G. Black, London 1921.
Norfolk and Suffolk Coast. W. A. Dutt. T. Fisher Unwin, London 1909.
History and Antiquities of the County of Norfolk. M. J. Armstrong. M. Booth, Norwich 1781.
White's *Directory of Norfolk* 1836.
History of Norfolk. W. Rye. Elliott Stock, London 1885.
White's *Directory of Suffolk* 1874.

LOCAL

Flamborough Village and Headland. Edited R. Fisher. William Andrews, Hull 1894.

History of the Spurn Lighthouses. G. de Boer. East Yorkshire Local History Society 1968.

History of Cromer. A. C. Savin. Rounce and Wortley, Holt 1937.

History of Ipswich. G. R. Clarke. S. Piper, Ipswich 1830.

Winterton Ness. J. A. Steers. Trans. Norfolk and Norwich Naturalist Society, 1953.

History of Yarmouth. A. Swinden. John Crouse, Norwich 1772.

Orford Ness—A Collection of Maps (mainly by John Norden). Presented to J. A. Steers. W. Heffer, Cambridge 1966.

Aldeburgh—The History of an Ancient Borough. H. P. Clodd. Norman Adlard, Ipswich 1959.

Alde Estuary. W. G. Arnott. The Boydell Press, Ipswich 1952.

A Brief History of Southwold Haven. E. R. Cooper. Frederick Jenkins, Southwold 1907.

History of Audley End. 3rd Lord Braybrooke 1836.

Audley End. W. Addison. J. M. Dent, London 1953.

History of the Borough of King's Lynn. Written and published by H. P. Hillen 1907.

The Port of King's Lynn. King's Lynn Conservancy Board, 1961.

History of Hunstanton. J. S. Cobb. Jarrold & Sons, London 1868.

Serjeant-Surgeon John Knight. E. M. & R. T. C. Calvert. William Heinemann (Medical Books), London 1939.

History of Harwich Harbour. B. Carlyon Hughes. The Standard Printing & Publishing Co, Dovercourt 1939.

The Story of Colchester. Geoffrey Martin. Benham Newspapers, Colchester 1959.

The Felixstowe Story. A. Jobson. Robert Hale, London 1968.

Lowestoft, East Coast Port. Robert Malster. Terence Dalton, Lavenham 1982.

Index

(Illustrations in **bold type**)

INDEX